D1158239

How to Achieve Zero-Defect Marketing

HF
5415.157
.M34
1993

How to Achieve Zero-Defect Marketing

Allan J. Magrath

GEORGE M. SMILEY MEMORIAL LIBRARY
CENTRAL METHODIST COLLEGE
FAYETTE, MISSOURI 65248

GEORGE M. SMILEY MEMORIAL LIBRARY
CENTRAL METHODIST COLLEGE
FAYETTE, MISSOURI 65248

amacom

American Management Association

New York • Atlanta • Boston • Chicago • Kansas City • San Francisco • Washington D.C.
Brussels • Toronto • Mexico City

This book is available at a special discount when ordered in bulk quantities. For information, contact Special Sales Department, AMACOM, a division of American Management Association, 135 West 50th Street, New York, NY 10020.

This publication is designed to provide accurate and authoritative information in regard to the subject matter covered. It is sold with the understanding that the publisher is not engaged in rendering legal, accounting, or other professional service. If legal advice or other expert assistance is required, the services of a competent professional person should be sought.

AMACOM Books, a division of American Management Association
135 West 50th Street, New York, NY 10020

This book is also distributed by: Quality Resources
A division of The Kraus Organization, Ltd.
One Water Street, White Plains, New York 10601
ISBN 0-527-76218-0

Library of Congress Cataloging-in-Publication Data
Magrath, Allan J.
How to achieve zero-defect marketing / Allan J. Magrath.
p. cm.
Includes bibliographical references and index.
ISBN 0-8144-5123-3
1. Quality of products. 2. Marketing. I. Title. II. Title:
Zero-defect marketing.
HF5415.157.M34   1993   92-42963
658.8'02—dc20   CIP

© 1993 Allan J. Magrath.
All rights reserved. Printed in the United States of America.

This publication may not be reproduced, stored in a retrieval system, or transmitted in whole or in part, in any form or by any means, electronic, mechanical, photocopying, recording, or otherwise, without the prior written permission of AMACOM, a division of American Management Association, 135 West 50th Street, New York, NY 10020.

Printing number

10 9 8 7 6 5 4 3 2 1

For
Virginia and Matthew,
all my love forever

Contents

Foreword

James A. Belasco, Ph.D.

Allan Magrath goes for the jugular. He attacks the two biggest challenges facing North American industry today: improving service productivity while providing significantly higher levels of service quality—*as defined by the customer*. He scores direct hits on both targets. His book, *How to Achieve Zero-Defect Marketing*, is an invaluable handbook for meeting the challenges of the new marketing in the rapidly approaching twenty-first century.

The Sorry State of Service Productivity

The figures are legion—and depressing. Service productivity remains stuck at the 1975 level. Productivity gains in the manufacturing sector obscure the lack of progress in the service sector. With the shift to a more service-based economy, the inability to raise service productivity promises to continue the stagnating standard of living throughout North America.

It's not for lack of trying. Billions of dollars in computerization and automation failed to move the needle. Intensive training programs in customer service and quality pass over the heads of jaded disbelieving employees. The more managers work to improve service productivity, the more productivity levels remain the same.

The Old Way Is No Longer THE Way

Spurred by the need to improve margins, many managers resort to the traditional management fixes of cost cutting, de-layering, slimming the product line, and disposing of unproductive assets. One round of cost cutting succeeds another with the all-too-familiar pattern of high expectations and promise followed by the same old dismal performance. All the while, employee loyalty fades, and customers go elsewhere. The old management nostrums aren't working.

The old management paradigm stresses the manager's responsibility to plan, organize, command, coordinate, and control, and assumes that the employees will go along. In Henri Fayol's and Max Weber's time, that paradigm worked well for managing the French coal mines or the nineteenth-century German army. It is considerably less effective today. Circumstances have changed; our paradigms have not. As a result, we are trapped in a time warp, applying nineteenth-century principles to twenty-first-century situations.

Management Mind-Sets Must Change

Magrath is absolutely correct. We must move from the traditional function-focused four-P marketing model to his more process-oriented seven-systems model based upon TQM principles. Specifically, three dramatic mind-set shifts are required: Reorganize around systemic process-management systems and structures, focus on employee productivity/satisfaction as the driver for service quality, and form both internal and external partnerships. Let's examine each in turn.

Reorganization Around Systemic Process Management Principles

Henri Fayol, Max Weber, and Frederick Taylor urged specialization and the functional division of management as the most efficient organization system. That system made sense in the later half of the nineteenth century, where the work force was largely uneducated, and focusing on a narrow task was necessary to achieve high levels of performance. Specialization splintered marketing activities into such diverse "professions" as: marketing research, distribution, logistics, provisioning, and sales. Serving customers became a series of increasingly difficult "handoffs," each running the risk of a fumble. In one organization, the process of filling a customer's order required more than 1,100 different steps, involving 262 interorganizational transfers. And they called their process "simplified implementation!" Not only did the cost of the system guarantee that they were the highest cost supplier, it also led to rigid and slow installations that produced customer satisfaction ratings below 20 percent. Talk about the worst of all worlds!

Rather than see the organization as a series of specialized functions, Magrath powerfully argues for viewing the organization as an integrated system designed to serve the customer. His TQM-based approach is right on the money! Furthermore, he gives many helpful ways to translate the systemic perspective into real-time marketing practice.

For too many marketing people, their profession is their prison; they can't see beyond their own four walls. In today's rapidly changing market, that perspective is a sure recipe for disaster. Marketers need to help everyone reach out beyond their walls and influence the *full stream* of activities necessary to satisfy their customers.

The literature is replete with examples where TQM-based systemic process management resulted in significant economic savings and dramatically improved customer service. One example in which I was personally involved resulted in a 29 percent cost reduction, a 62 percent reduction in sales-installation cycle time, a 47 percent increase in customer satisfaction scores, and a gain in nine market share points. All this was accomplished through reorganizing by three major processes: strategy formulation, product realization, and product distribution. The sales department became the process owner and driver of the product-distribution process. Local sales teams were responsible for delivering and installing products developed and manufactured in worldwide product-realization facilities, where the original sales-install cycle averaged twenty-seven months. To execute their new responsibilities, people discovered that they needed to redesign their processes, which they did using TQM principles.

How you reorganize is crucial, however. Given today's work force, top-down–driven reorganizations, even if to a process-management system, will likely result in continued organizational underperformance. That leads to the next point.

Focusing on Employee Productivity/Satisfaction as the Driver for Service Quality

In the example above, the president organized multilevel, multilocation, multifunctional teams drawn from those currently involved in the process. Overall, more than seven percent of the work force was involved in the process and organizational redesign. Furthermore, no process was changed or department reorganized until everyone involved had the opportunity to comment on the change.

The president's actions reflected the following value equation:

FINANCIAL RESULTS

CUSTOMER SATISFACTION

EMPLOYEE PRODUCTIVITY/SATISFACTION

Most managers in the old paradigm focus on financial results, spending hours pouring over budgets and plans. One survey discovered that managers spent 78 percent of their time working with budgeting and planning data. Yet an overwhelming amount of research, based on the PIMS and other data, indicates that financial results (particularly in terms of long-term margins and market share) are a direct result of customer satisfaction.

Recent data demonstrate that customer satisfaction, in turn, is a reflection of employee satisfaction. Satisfied employees are the principle producers of customer satisfaction, which, in turn, is the principle determiner of financial results. One caveat, however: Seventy years of research fails to identify any consistent relationship between satisfaction and productivity. Contented cows do not give more or better milk. The only consistent finding is that people who are more productive are more satisfied. Thus, the emphasis must be on creating the conditions where employees feel productive. Productivity has a dual meaning: First is the feeling that "I made a difference," and second is customer feedback, which validates the reality that "I did make a difference." Thus, managers need to shift focus from planning and budgeting to creating the environment where people feel—and are—productive for their customers.

Managing the Context to Create Employee Productivity/Satisfaction. Magrath correctly points out that marketers must change the systems and structures to encourage this employee ownership of the new TQM process-management paradigm. In one organization, the marketing department received all customer complaint letters. The marketing people sent out good answers. That wasn't the problem. That system, however, insulated the people who designed, made, and/or shipped the product from knowing what customers thought of their actions. Simply by changing the system and sending the letters directly to the people involved in the product realization process, they saw, for the first time, what turned customers on and off. Now product realization people work with product distribution people to handle customer problems. The people on the production line, for instance, respond to complaint letters and do whatever is necessary to satisfy that customer. To prevent complaint letters, production workers now measure product quality and use these measurements to improve production processes. This simple system change (connecting people with direct customer feedback) reflects the marketing staff's systemic process-management approach, which extends their influence beyond their office walls. Their actions (modifying systems so that people can add value throughout the entire product realization/product distribution chain) is the future of marketing.

Forming Partnerships With Customers

Magrath scores another direct hit in identifying the need to move from a selling approach to a partnership approach with customers. The selling game is old and well known: "Sell, sell, sell." When times get tough, the message is simple: "Sell, sell, sell, more!" Experience confirms Magrath's thesis that the best way to sell is through building partnerships with customers. Consider the following anecdote from a sales manager.

> I always practiced the *sales* approach. In the ink business, it was very clear. "Let me tell you why black is the best color," I trained my salespeople to say. "It looks great on the paper. It conveys an image of power and control. It's relatively inexpensive." I made my living selling features and benefits. Then customers became more

sophisticated. There were more choices in the marketplace. Competitors got smarter.

In an effort to stay ahead of the pack, I changed my tune. "What color would you like?" I trained my salespeople to ask their customers. We adopted a more *customer-orientated* approach. If a customer wanted pink-perfumed ink, we'd mix them up a batch. If the customer wanted it next Tuesday, we'd get it to them next Tuesday. That worked for a while. But, as usual, times changed. Customers got even more sophisticated. Competitors got even smarter. We had to change or run the risk of being buried.

Now I train my salespeople to say. "Let's work *together* to discover how color can contribute to *your* goals." Now we have a *partnership* approach. We've shifted our emphasis from what we have in the bag (or can get from the factory) to what the customer needs. My job now is not to sell my products; it's to help the customer achieve his/her goals, and I get everyone's help throughout the company in doing it.

Customers Are Where Marketing Begins— and Ends

Nothing happens until somebody buys something. That's why customers need to be marketing's central focus. Most of all, marketing must be about helping everyone in the organization to own the responsibility to get and keep customers. Every person, every day must view every activity, every procedure, every process through the perspective of: "How does this contribute to serving my customer?" Each and every person must own the responsibility for delighting customers. Magrath's TQM approach is central to achieving this goal.

At a process-managed sausage company, they know what their customers want: great taste and fun using their products. Everyone in the company is focused on producing great taste every time. Their production people track and chart every day's production of every product. They compare it to the competition. They compare it to their customer-taste profiles. They study their customers for clues on how to make their products even better. They are continuously working on new technologies that will revolutionize the industry. This is part of a never-ending drive to create the ultimate taste experience for their customers. Ask any person who works in that company, "What's the top priority?" and they will answer, "Making great-tasting sausage."

What customers want is different for every company. People probably won't stand in line for great-tasting airplanes. That means there are no recipes. Marketing's job is to focus everyone in the company on owning the responsibility to find out what their customers want—and then on consistently delivering it. In doing that, we will solve the twin problems of poor service-productivity and low service-quality levels. Magrath shows us how to use TQM principles to hit a home run in improving our individual, organizational, and societal standards of living.

How to Achieve Zero-Defect Marketing

1

A Process Mind-Set for Marketers

The inefficiency in manufacturing performance often lies less with the individual than with the system in which he or she functions—this same situation exists in systems engaged in by service or knowledge workers.

Dr. Mitchell Rabkin, President,
Beth Israel Hospital, New York*

Many of today's biggest breakthroughs in management practice are occurring as the result of the application of a "process" mind-set to corporate functions. As the opening quotation so eloquently states, systems—rather than individuals—often determine efficiency, whether in manufacturing or in service functions such as marketing. A process mind-set is also critical for any company or department that is striving for continuous improvement, or total quality management (TQM).

To date, however, few marketers have taken advantage of this way of looking at their performance. Focusing on process—developing a systems-oriented outlook—offers a golden opportunity for marketers to achieve total quality throughout the marketing cycle. Business process redesign allows marketing to get closer to the optimal value equation: that which drives benefits up and costs down. This is what I call Zero-Defect Marketing.

*In a letter to the editor, *Harvard Business Review,* January-February 1992.

Process Breakthroughs

Both manufacturing and service companies have witnessed dramatic success by applying a process mind-set to particular functions. In manufacturing, for instance, Toyota, now the most profitable company in the auto industry, pioneered the Just-In-Time (J-I-T) production process for automotive assembly. According to a 1991 article in *Business Week*, compared to General Motors' ten units per employee, Toyota's system produces forty-eight units per employee. And it takes only thirteen man-hours of labor per car versus twenty-two hours at General Motors. J-I-T has allowed Toyota to operate with fewer people, lower overhead, and less inventory, making better margins per car.

McDonald's restaurants, a leader in the fast-food service industry, applied a process improvement mind-set to its purchasing system with startling results. In 1970 its needs were supplied by some 200 independent distributors, each providing its own narrow product line to franchised stores. Each McDonald's franchise acted as an independent buying unit, separately negotiating purchases from each distributor for 200–300 items. As a result, a franchise would receive twenty-five deliveries per store per week and would hold significant in-store inventories, such as a month's supply of frozen hamburger patties. This process created unacceptable quality variances in the food delivered and was burdensome to the franchise's financial cash flow. McDonald's took a look at the process and decided to partner with fewer suppliers and organize its franchises into regional cooperative buying units.

With tighter supplier partnering, McDonald's encouraged the fewer distributors to offer more value-added services. In 1990, 85 percent of McDonald's U.S. store needs were served by just four large distributors (each of which supplied 300+ products). The remaining 15 percent of needs were supplied by ten other smaller distributors. Thus, a process improvement mind-set cut distributors from 200 in 1970 to 14 in 1990. These fewer distributors made only three batch deliveries per store per week from a master once-a-week order. In this way, distribution costs to McDonald's were reduced by 20 percent and store inventories by 60 percent. Quality variances have been minimized. Distributors offer value-added services such as calculating optimum order mixes for stores on the basis of historic selling patterns, and the regional cooperatives have greater buying clout and control over pricing from these fewer distributors than did individual franchises.

A process mind-set, when applied to a management function, allows for the flow charting of where delays occur and costs pile up. For instance, in a manufacturing setting, traditional batch models looked at lead times as a series of steps, such as transit time, queuing time, set-up time, run time, and waiting time. A process cycle-time mind-set sees the manufacturing operation as delay + delay + delay + run + delay. A process mind-set focused on cycle time examines all steps that may be normal activities but are nonetheless nonessential. A process orientation doesn't just look at improving the time management of individual tasks in a process; it focuses on reducing the *total* cycle time, in many cases by eliminating nonessential steps or by running them simultaneously rather than sequentially.

Figure 1-1 outlines functions of corporations in which major process breakthroughs have occurred. These process breakthroughs have led to system redesigns that bring products to market faster, cut waste in production, improve quality, cut part numbers, reduce warranty claims, and boost worker knowledge and productivity. Figure 1-2 shows these results.

Process Improvements in Marketing

Marketing can also benefit greatly from process redesign and change. This is the case whether marketing's thrust is to improve only one part of its interlinked systems or several parts at once.

Figure 1-3 illustrates how each of the seven key systems of marketing is connected to the other and how all comprise a subset of the compay's overall market planning/research system.

The seven key systems can be briefly described as follows:

1. The company's *persuasion system*, using various media, persuades potential customers or existing customers to purchase or rebuy the company's offerings. This involves the promotion, advertising, packaging design, and publicity functions of the company as well as its corporate identity campaign.

Figure 1-1. Process breakthroughs.

Manufacturing	○ Improved materials flow Just-In-Time
	○ Advanced process technologies, e.g., robotics, vision systems, cellular plant layouts
	○ Statistical process control
	○ Computer-assisted manufacturing
	○ Restructuring: focused factories
	○ Factory resource improvements: preventive maintenance; cross-trained work teams (self-managed)
	○ Simultaneous engineering
Customer Service	○ Electronic data interchange (EDI)
	○ Toll-free complaint handling
	○ Built-in machine service diagnostics
Logistics	○ Bar coding of stock-keeping units
	○ Automated warehousing
	○ Material requirements planning (MRP)
Purchasing	○ Vendor certification/qualification
	○ Vendor partnerships/sole sourcing
	○ Contract systems

2. The company's *selling system* includes its field account coverage methods and its sales force management practices.

3. The *incentivizing system* entices resellers or customers to purchase the company's products or services via its pricing schedules, its terms of payment, its volume discounts, its rebate levels, its special offers, coupons, and other forms of price inducements.

4. The *product innovation system* generates new products (and services) to help the marketer grow or replace aging offerings. Research and development is the key part of this system.

5. The corporation's *marketing channel system* makes use of wholesalers, retailers, dealers, agents, or other resellers to assist its own selling system in servicing demand and developing the market.

6. The *logistics and customer service system* facilitates the customer's ordering and delivery needs. This also involves a myr-

Figure 1-2. Results of process redesign.

Faster time to market

Part number reductions

Better quality — continuous improvement

Lower reliance on need for warranties

Knowledge workers

Cross-functional teams — internal

Lower waste levels

Pushed-down costs

iad of subsystems, including transportation, warehousing, order expediting, assortment bundling, labeling, and invoicing activities.

7. The *market planning and research system* looks at customers and competitors in an effort to prioritize opportunities or threats to the company's current and future offerings (of products/ services). The company's competitive intelligence system and market research gathering are key components of the planning process used by the company to benchmark its market position/ share, to identify market segments, competitor strongholds, market growth, and other environmental factors occurring in the market.

Like the respiratory system, digestive system, nervous system, or circulatory system in the human body, these systems all work together holistically to confer marketing "health" on a company. When any part is improved, healthy marketing follows; when several parts are improved at once, even more healthy results follow in the marketplace.

For instance, Apple Computer has worked on improving three of these seven systems in Japan. It has improved its product inno-

Figure 1-3. The multiple systems of marketing.

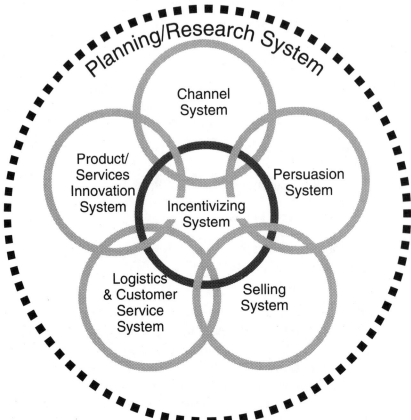

vation system by making its Macintosh computers run on Japanese-language software. To distribute its computers, it has boosted its channel system capacity by making deals with five major Japanese companies—Minolta, Sharp Electronics, Mitsubishi, Brother Industries, and Kokuyo (a leader in office stationery). At the same time, Apple has improved its marketing persuasion by creating a stronger brand image for Apple products by way of hip promotions of Apple-licensed T-shirts, coffee mugs, and key chains at such high-profile events as the Japanese Ladies' Professional Golf Tournament and at Japanese rock concerts featuring pop star entertainers like Janet Jackson. These three system improvements raised

Apple's share from one percent in 1988 to 6 percent by 1991 and sales of Macs from 55,000 per year to 180,000 per year in this same time frame.[1]

Some companies hone in on only one part of their marketing for major process gains. Amp, the world's preeminent maker of electrical and electronic connectors, has concentrated on redesigning its selling system to emphasize major customer partnerships. It has solidified relationships between its sales engineers and the product designers at its key customers. As a result, it has been successful in becoming the sole source of supply for connectors with several huge clients—General Electric's ($5.4-billion) Appliance Division; Auto Latina, the Ford-Volkswagen joint venture in Brazil; and Boeing, where Amp works with Boeing to design many of its electronic control systems. Amp's marketing health has greatly improved, with its market share at 18 percent globally—four times greater than its closest rival's.[2] Church & Dwight Company, makers of Arm & Hammer baking soda, concentrates efforts on product innovation to continually find new uses for its bicarbonate of soda. It has been moved from baking use to air freshener, carpet deodorizer, water additive, and even to a sandblasting agent. (The Statue of Liberty was sandblasted with it in 1986.)

Phillips-VanHeusen, the dress shirt maker, has sought innovation in its channel system by expanding distribution from department stores only to more than 200 factory outlets. As a result, VanHeusen's share of the market, at 9.9 percent, surpassed Arrow's, its long-time rival, for the first time in 1992 (Arrow is at 9.2 percent market share).[3]

VISA has not tried to improve on its products/services or selling/channel systems so much as redirected its advertising and promotion dollars. Its emphasis has been to alter its marketing persuasion system to go after the loyalty of resellers of its VISA credit cards and VISA traveler's checks, while its rival, American Express, has concentrated on advertising directly to travelers. VISA's altered persuasion system has paid off; its share of the credit card business is up, and sales of its traveler's checks have risen by $2.1 billion while American Express's business volume has shrunk by this same amount.

Sometimes, as a company works to improve one of its key marketing processes, it experiences positive and unanticipated spin-off effects. As various hotel chains have experimented with discount price packages to improve their incentivizing systems, they have found or tapped new, growing market niches. This has happened with the Hyatt, Four Seasons, and Hilton chains, each of which has experimented with special pricing for grandparent weekends, single-parent outings, weekends with teenagers, and so forth. Some of these discounts have attracted so much interest that the chains have now spun them off as parts of complete marketing campaigns. Hyatt offers day-care camp for kids, and one hotel, Ambassador East in Chicago, now offers "VIPet" treatment, in which a guest and his or her pet are pampered with doggie-bag meals and pet exercise and grooming services.

The Benefits of Understanding Marketing Systems

By breaking marketing practice down into systems, marketing people can get the same sort of leverage and quality improvements as have proved possible in manufacturing, engineering, and purchasing.

For instance, consider Microsoft, the world's largest software company. Microsoft, by concentrating on its product innovation system, has been able to get its products to market *faster*. And in a fast-paced market where customer learning is critical, being first with new software means that customers are often unwilling to switch once they have spent hours learning your product. As a result of its Windows program being first to market, Microsoft has a 72 percent share of the spreadsheet market, 44 percent in word processing, and 16 percent in presentation graphics (1992—U.S. shares).[4] The stock market has rewarded Microsoft by capitalizing its stock at $21 billion in value, forty-seventh among the world's top one hundred companies. Clearly, the concentration on its product innovation system gave it fast cycle time in a market where this is a telling advantage.

Process improvements in marketing systems almost invariably lower costs, boost responsiveness, lower waste in spending, and improve teamwork, all key planks in Zero-Defect Marketing.

For instance, General Mills, in entering a joint venture distribution arrangement with Nestlé to sell its cereals outside North

America (Cereal Partners Worldwide), saved $200 million in start-up marketing costs that it would otherwise have had to spend to get shelf space for its cereal brands in markets where Nestlé already had the contacts and clout with European grocers. General Mills found great leverage on its costs by concentrating on a novel improvement in its channel system, that is, by taking on an established, well-connected retail partner.

Hewlett-Packard has concentrated on its product innovation system's cycle time and can now produce products such as its spectrum analyzer in half the time at half the cost it once did. As a result, it has a 75 percent global share in this industry, including the tough Japanese market.

Baxter International, the $8.9-billion hospital products company, has managed to wring the waste out of the hospital supply chain by paying attention to its logistics and customer service system. It invested in a Value Link information service that ties its hospital customers' order needs electronically to its own warehouses. Value Link provides complete and instant feedback on hospital reorder needs by hospital department location. Baxter's system has saved some hospitals both inventory and administration costs that often total $17,000 to $20,000 per month. And this cost reduction to hospitals has been accompanied by no loss in on-time accurate order fulfillment, that is, quality zero-defect performance.[5]

Japan has the lowest-cost, most efficient channel system in the world for soft drinks because vending has been developed as a stronger channel than in the United States. Fully half of its $24 billion in retail soft drinks is dispensed via vending versus only 10 percent in the United States.

A New Mind-Set for Marketers

Of course, concentrating on system performance variables such as waste, cycle time, flexibility, unit cost, and customer satisfaction calls for a newer, slightly different, and "richer" marketer mind-set than that in which marketers are focused on discrete tasks or macro results such as market share, growth in revenue, or profitability.

Figure 1-4 models this needed paradigm shift in the mar-

Figure 1-4. The paradigm mind-set shift required of marketers.

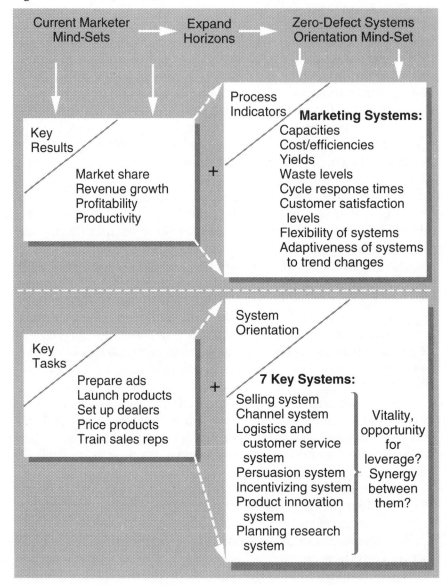

keter's mind-set and tool kit. As the figure illustrates, marketing based on a whole system's perspective teaches a new language and changes its orientation from a focus on the professionalism or proficiency of its efforts to a focus on a broadened array of measurements and analytical tools.

In many organizations, marketing has always concentrated on proficiency in program design and execution. Marketing views its performance in terms of the professionalism or elegance of its programs and often overlooks or downplays other, less obvious process variables such as yield, responsiveness, unit cost, or waste. Marketers can be single-minded in the pursuit of professional selling, slick ad campaigns, polished brand creations, clever market segmentation, attractive and eye-catching packaging, motivational incentive contests, and so forth. In many organizations, this focus on discrete activities (as opposed to the whole system) has meant that the coordinated integration of all marketing systems has been suboptimal. Product managers may concoct promotions that neither the sales function nor the production function can execute well. Salespeople may demand backup help that marketing cannot provide expeditiously. Marketing and sales often operate in two solitudes, sometimes not even reporting to the same manager. Marketing may also not team as well as it might with the lab (on new product development) or with customer service (on order-handling issues or complaint handling) or with production scheduling. In more process-oriented management functions such as manufacturing or purchasing, the personnel recognize that they operate systems with interdependent parts. They know that it is possible for the world's four fastest runners to lose a relay race if their baton transfers are poor. These sorts of corporate functions look at the total time from start to finish (or total system costs) and not just at the individual performance of the system's components. Marketing often remains stubbornly focused on individual task components or people rather than on its total system.

By shifting its orientation to a broader array of systems and system outputs, marketers can engineer changes that lead to much higher customer satisfaction and responsiveness. This is somewhat analogous to motor sports. Those world-class racing teams that consistently win Grand Prix races or other championships have both well-oiled teamwork among the drivers, owners, and pit crews and a culture to continually measure the car's many system outputs—for example, clutch wear, tire wear, brake wear, engine temperature, gear box efficiency, horsepower, lap speed, suspension, and steering performance. By practicing more teamwork with other functions and by measuring and understanding their company's various systems, marketers can find new ways to engineer changes that benefit customers.

By overhauling all its various marketing systems (and in the process becoming very marketing-driven), Reynolds Metals Co. has defeated steel companies in a whole host of markets from auto and appliance parts to beverage cans, boat hulls, and grain bins, while giving the world newly pioneered aluminum products for roofing, windows, siding, and even baseball bats. Reynolds has priced its products on the basis of perceived customer value, increased its channels, educated its customers to its products' uniqueness, been the first to emphasize recycling in advertising copy, and passed any lower-cost factory efficiencies on to its best customers. Once-loyal steel customers became newly loyal aluminum customers. As a result, a comparison of its fortunes with those of a company such as Bethlehem Steel shows a marked contrast. Bethlehem's sales outpaced Reynolds' six to one in 1975, yet by 1990 Reynolds sales exceeded $6 billion while Bethlehem's were below the $5-billion level. And Reynolds made a profit of $450 million for 1990 and 1991 combined versus a loss for Bethlehem of $1.23 billion! Today Reynolds is 34 percent larger than Bethlehem in 1992, and its work force is growing, as is its customer base. Bethlehem continues to shutter factories and shrink its work force.

A total focus on its marketing systems from product innovation to incentivizing, selling, channel, and persuasion systems has paid off big for Reynolds in the market.

System Subcomponents

Succeeding chapters take the marketing systems paradigm further by delineating the component parts of each system and then suggesting some ways to redesign or alter them for the benefit of customers or the company's own efficiency.

A sample flowchart of a marketing persuasion system is illustrated in Figure 1-5.

Figure 1-5. A persuasion system flowchart of major components.

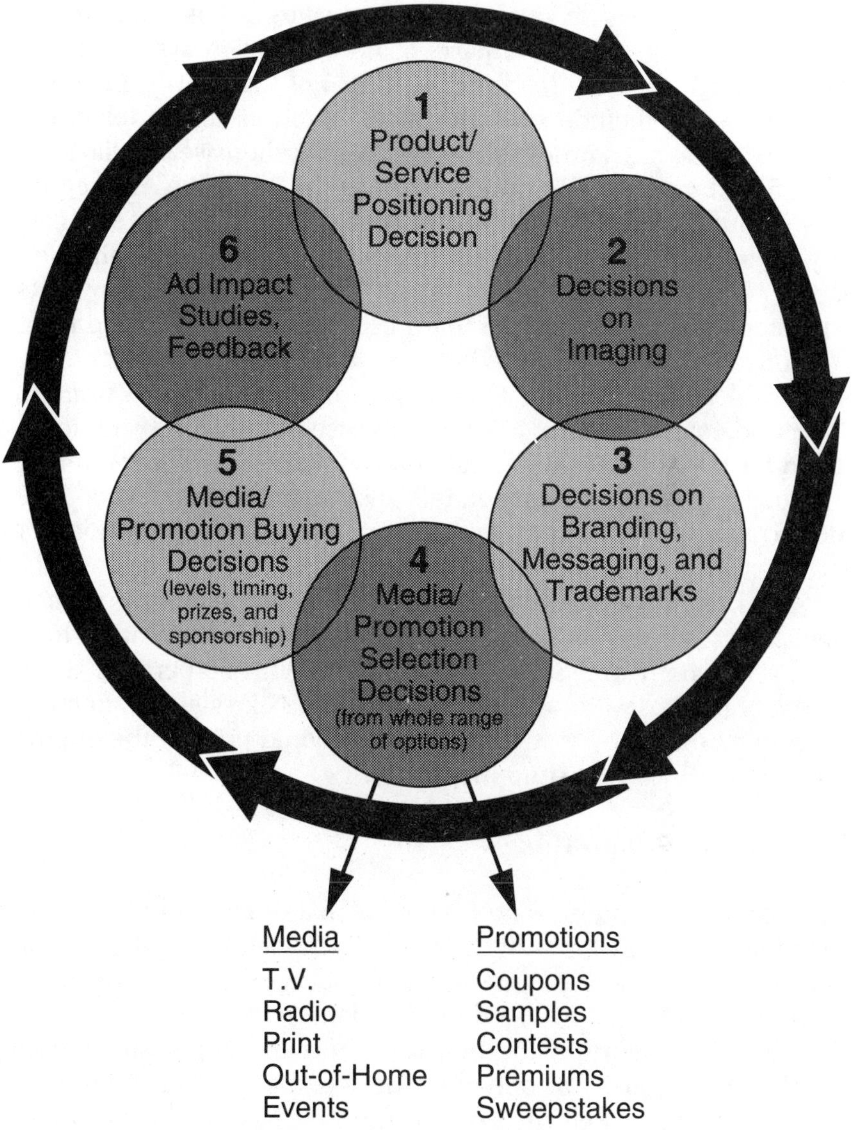

Media	Promotions
T.V.	Coupons
Radio	Samples
Print	Contests
Out-of-Home	Premiums
Events	Sweepstakes

Nike has pioneered system changes in several parts of its persuasion system. For example, in recent years it has made major emphasis changes in three parts of its persuasion system: (1) it has expanded the *variety* of media (step 4 of Figure 1-5) in which it advertises to include specialty media such as music television (MTV); (2) it has launched *globally* comprehensive media buys (step 5) to launch new products such as the 180 Nike Air jogging shoe (simultaneously advertised in nineteen of the world's largest city markets spread out over North America, Europe, Australia, and Japan); and (3) it is changing the copy and imagery in many of its ads (step 2) to reach out to women because Nike discovered from ad impact studies (step 6) that ads featuring endorsements by such athletes as Michael Jordan were of no interest to women. Newer ad copy appeals to a woman's sense of self. For example, in its ad for the Nike Air Essential shoe (walking shoes for women), the copy addresses how women feel about their bodies. It says: YOU ARE NOT A GODDESS . . . BUT JUST BECAUSE YOU ARE HUMAN DOESN'T MEAN WE CAN'T WORSHIP THE GROUND YOU WALK ON.

As a result of Nike's marketing persuasion changes, women now constitute 15 percent of its sales (up from 5 percent), which is a lot of money in a $3-billion company. With 50 percent of the potential market worldwide among women, Nike's efforts to reengineer one of its key marketing systems could provide the engine for its growth for years into the future.[6]

The Quality Connection

In upcoming chapters, each system of marketing will be held up to the light to show how changes in its components can lead to big boosts in corporate performance and quality. Systems analysis in marketing and TQM fit together like Siamese twins.

Doing things right the first time in marketing systems pays very big dividends. Not only does the company avoid the wasted resources that created the error in the first place; it saves the resources it takes to find the problem, and the added resources it takes to fix it. Zero-Defect Marketing suggests a new paradigm of marketing behavior: It asks marketers to shift from the four *p*'s of products, price, promotion, and place (distribution) to seven systems; it asks marketers to look at how these systems actually work and at how they *can* work to heighten system yields, cut costs, lower waste, and provide long-term customer satisfaction in the tough decade of the 1990s.

Notes

1. Neil Gross and Kathy Rebello, "Apple? Japan Can't Say NO," *Business Week* (June 29, 1991), pp. 32–33.
2. Andrew Erdman, "Amp Staying Ahead of Competitors," *Fortune* (June 1, 1992), pp. 111–112.
3. "Van-Heusen's Share Surpasses Arrow's," *The Wall Street Journal* (May 22, 1992), pp. B1, B5.
4. G. McWilliams, K. Rebello, and Evan Schwartz, "The PC Price Wars Are Sweeping Into Software," *Business Week* (July 13, 1992), p. 132.
5. Susan Caminiti, "Finding New Ways to Sell More," *Fortune* (July 27, 1992), p. 102.
6. Ibid., p. 101. Also see Geraldine E. Willigan, "High Performance Marketing: An Interview with Nike's Phil Knight," *Harvard Business Review* (July-August 1992), pp. 90–101.

2

The Persuasion System

Let's say you are a manufacturer. Your advertising isn't working, and your sales are going down—and everything depends on it. And you walk in this office—Do you want glowing things that can be framed by copywriters? Or do you want to see the sales curve stop moving down and start moving up?

Rosser Reeves
Legendary ad man
The former Ted Bates Ad Agency*

Chapter 1, in introducing the subject of processes and their components, illustrated one sample marketing process—that of the company's marketing persuasion process.

As we have seen, the marketing persuasion system fits into the total marketing system as illustrated in Figure 1-3. Companies use a variety of media, promotions, and publicity programs to persuade potential customers to buy and rebuy their products or services. These could include electronic media (such as radio or television), print media (such as magazines or newspapers), specialized media (such as trade shows), and out-of-home media (such as billboards or point-of-sale), as well as the entire range of promotional media from sampling, contests, and sweepstakes to coupons, premiums, and factory rebates. Publicity initiatives can range from publicity releases, press conferences, and third-party testimonials to the sponsorship of large events such as the Olympics. Each of these major persuasion areas involves the complex of decisions originally outlined in Figure 1-5, namely the manage-

*In his book *Reality in Advertising*.

ment of images, brands, media selection, buying, and measurement.

For consumer companies selling packaged goods, spending on persuasion systems can consume up to 30–35 percent of their total sales dollars, as was the case with Alberto-Culver in 1990. By contrast, industrial company spending may be more modest, probably below 10 percent of sales, because industrial concerns often spend comparatively more money on their selling systems or channel systems (sales force, field management, distributor supports). Nonetheless, spending on marketing persuasion is often significant, and if decreased through better process management, big gains in bottom-line profits are possible. In addition, since persuasion systems often involve the management of brand assets to obtain the highest possible brand equity, process improvement thinking also holds out the promise of better asset yields from brands. Enlightened brand management can often provide a company with a product having a long life cycle. For instance, Oreo cookies are an eighty-year-old brand, first brought to market in 1912. Even in the toy industry, renowned for fad products with short life cycles, some brands have been extremely well managed for many years and still sell well sometimes thirty to forty or even seventy-five years after their introduction.

Here are the names of ten such toy products and the years in which they were introduced:

Toy Product	Year Introduced
1. Crayola Crayons (Binney & Smith)	1903
2. Raggedy Ann and Andy (Hasbro)	1915
3. Playskool Alphabet Blocks	1917
4. Lego Building Blocks	1930
5. Monopoly (Parker Brothers)	1935
6. Tonka Trucks	1946
7. Mr. Potato Head (Hasbro)	1952
8. Play Doh (Kenner)	1955
9. Barbie (Mattel)	1959
10. Ohio Art's Etch a Sketch	1960

In industrial markets, 3M and Black & Decker have sustained many brands with long life cycles. 3M's reflective sign material for highway signs—branded Scotchlite—is over fifty years old, while Black & Decker's drills date back several decades.

The Variables That Count Most in Optimum Persuasion System Management

The key to managing a persuasion system for continuous improvement is to focus on lowering waste in media spending while choosing media with high flexibility so that they can be targeted and scheduled flexibly. Promotional vehicles should be gauged for efficiency, that is, by how much yield they produce per dollar expended. For instance, how many coupons are redeemed compared with the cost expended to distribute each? In the area of the persuasion system involving imaging creation, messaging creation, or positioning choices, the focus must be on producing images, brands, trademarks, slogans, and theme lines having high impact (yield as measured by target customer awareness or recall scores) with a minimum of false starts. Because the creative development of brand images and advertising is often the purview of advertising agencies, it is therefore crucial to select and manage an agency on the basis both of the impact of the creative work it produces and the management finesse with which it does this. Creative advertising that costs too much, is late for a ready market, or is incomplete in some way will detract from all other parts of the entire persuasion system—from the promotions that tie into it to the media purchased to give voice to its message. Agencies must produce good copy on a just-in-time basis that can build and sustain an identity for a brand over time. Burger King, over a period of eight years, had six different creative campaigns, which greatly damaged its brand position by confusing its target audience about what the restaurant chain's products stood for. As a result, Burger King lost market share to other fast food chains that had more consistent imaging, such as McDonald's, Pizza Hut, and Taco Bell.

In general, it makes sense to conceptualize persuasion systems as a two-part equation. The first part involves managing creative elements, while the second part involves buying media in which to air these creative messages. The best persuasion systems emphasize a sensible balance in spending between these two. Too little money spent up front to arrive at compelling and attractive ads may greatly weaken a company's brand potency, while too much money spent perfecting the creative may leave insufficient funds to decisively deliver the message in print, on television, or through other media. Recall and ad awareness are greatly influenced by both creative content—the attention-getting power of the advertising—*and* the sheer weight of messaging, because messages must be repeated often to hit home with busy, fragmented target consumers. Memorable ad campaigns such as Duracell's battery commercials (IT'S THE COPPER-TOPPED BATTERY THAT LASTS AND LASTS) have had a durable impact on brand awareness for years after being aired.

In addition to the need for balance in spending between the creative elements and media buying, it is a sound rule of thumb to coordinate advertising, promotion, and public relations spending and effort so that a certain amount of overlap occurs. This is akin to the rule in the military to coordinate firepower on targets from a variety of sources so as to ensure successful target strikes. Bombers, artillery, and off-shore naval batteries all coordinate their fire to hit the target. Similarly, Taco Bell's spending on a television campaign in a local market ought to dovetail with its local coupon drop or any local event it is sponsoring.

Figure 2-1 illustrates the most important variables in a persuasion system.

Creative Impact

All high-impact creative advertising has certain features in common. All use imagery, trademarks, messages, and a good brand name in support of a benefit that the target customer values and that is most strongly represented by the brand as against competing brands. In essence, all good advertising has differentiating power to help a brand rise above its competitors. It is, however, the responsibility of the brand's holder, not its agency, to decide the differentiating dimension on which the competition will be waged. For instance, it is Maytag, not its agency, that chooses to differentiate its appliances on the basis of their durability. The agency's role is to guide the company in finding creative images and copy (such as the Maytag repairman waiting for service calls that never

Figure 2-1. Process variables that count in a persuasion system.

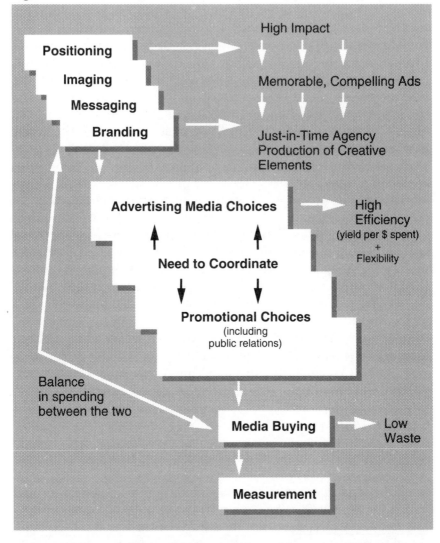

come!) that convey this point of difference in a memorable way. Media choices clearly condition the content of advertising in that television as a medium has the ability to convey a message that differs substantially from what could be conveyed over the radio, in a magazine, or on a billboard.

In the 1980s, brand differentiation weakened in many product categories as companies opted for allowing their agencies to use emotional appeals rather than more practical appeals to differentiate their products. As a result, consumers had a harder time knowing what the different brands really stood for, since the appeals to purchase them were very intangible. Thus, between 1986 and April 1991, brand loyalty among consumers slipped from 56 percent to 46 percent, as measured by the Roper Organization.[1]

When brands no longer stood out as clearly from one another, brand switching increased within product categories, and more private-label store brands were purchased in a trend that one industry observer has called "the commoditization of American packaged goods."[2] In addition, economically hard-pressed consumers began to reexamine the price-value equation of favorite brands with a more critical eye on the price part of that equation. Brands found wanting were often deemphasized in favor of the "value" brand. Any time a brand with strong differentiating power combined that power with a low price, it usually dominated its category. For instance, L'Eggs pantyhose did this and captured a 54 percent share of its market. Kellogg's, which had strong brands but insisted on raising prices as often as it could, suffered in share as its price-value eroded. Its cereal share fell from 42 percent in 1986 to 37 percent in 1991. It bounced back to a 39 percent share only after it began heavy supermarket couponing, which helped improve the price attractiveness of buying its cereals.[3]

Since differentiating combines both the choice of a brand's "unique selling proposition" and the advertising chosen to convey it, let's examine what constitutes excellence in differentiating impact.

Consider six leading brands, each of which has strong differentiating power: Maytag appliances, Timex watches, Heinz ketchup, Michelin tires, Kodak film, and Federal Express overnight courier service.

The first thing that is excellent about each of these brands is how clearly and consistently it has positioned itself to stand for some distinctive strength. Maytag and Timex have both positioned themselves on reliability. Heinz and Kodak are positioned on quality. Michelin is positioned as the best and safest tire, while Federal Express positions itself on speed and the guarantee that it will always deliver on its promised timing.

It is notable that each of these brands also has voracious competitors: Kodak against Fuji; Michelin versus Goodyear; Maytag versus Whirlpool or General Electric; Heinz versus Hunt's and store brands; Timex versus Seiko and dozens of others; Federal Express versus Purolator, United Parcel Service, and many other regional companies. What helps these leading brands to stand out is their high-impact advertising and the clever way it conveys their point of superiority/difference in the marketplace.

Maytag uses a vivid image of the loneliest repairman, always awaiting a call to fix their machines but never needing to do this. This imagery is more than thirty years old and still works in television ads, print ads, and dealer showroom ads.

Timex uses the slogan IT TAKES A LICKING AND IT KEEPS ON TICKING to demonstrate reliability. In the early years, television delivered the message in graphically demonstrative "torture tests" of the watches. In today's print ads, the company uses pictures and stories of everyday people who have experienced incredible mishaps and endured—each of whom wears a Timex. For a while, Timex lost its share because its product line went stale and was not considered contemporary in design. But when it got its product line back into a contemporary mode, it was able to resurrect its long-time slogan and make products such as its Timex "Sports Watch" a best-seller.

Heinz has chosen quality as its point of difference. This is a pretty generic sort of differentiating dimension in that everyone uses it. But Heinz's ads have had high impact because quality is illustrated by the THICKNESS, RICHNESS, AND TASTINESS of its ketchup; it's so thick, rich, and tasty it pours very slowly from the bottle, but its taste makes it worth the wait.

Kodak film has conveyed quality in numerous ways—by its bright yellow box, by its Olympic sponsorships, which connect it with excellence, and, most of all, by ads that convey the same constancy of message and imagery: YOU WOULDN'T WANT TO TRUST YOUR PRECIOUS MEMORIES TO ANY OTHER FILM THAN KODAK.

Michelin has chosen the vivid imagery of a baby seated inside its tires to convey the message that when you drive on Michelin tires your family will be driving on the world's safest—so you're really buying peace of mind. To back up this promise even further,

Michelin now offers an 80,000-mile tire-wear guarantee, the finest and longest in the tire industry.

Federal Express conveys its promise of speed with one of the world's most memorable slogans: WHEN IT ABSOLUTELY POSITIVELY HAS TO GET THERE OVERNITE. Its ad story lines consistently emphasize this speed dimension, whether picturing the "fast talker" or frustrated individuals sitting in stalled meetings kicking themselves for not using Fed Ex to be absolutely certain of getting their overnight package in time for their meeting.

Advertising techniques naturally vary among these top-branders, and even their media choices are different (for instance, Michelin uses very little television), but each has developed a clear brand identity through a combination of vivid imagery, pointed tag lines, memorable stories, or compelling symbols.

One newer approach to branding and brand image creation is to create an image around an umbrella brand that represents multiple products. Con Agra Inc. did this with Healthy Choice, a brand that stands for food products in the frozen food section for the health-conscious. Underneath this core brand identity, Con Agra has successfully marketed frozen dinners, breakfasts, baked goods, and even ice cream.

Line-extending brands, however, can be a two-edged sword. For every Con Agra example, there are dozens of companies that have tried to extend a brand too far, with disastrous results. Clorox spent $225 million to convince consumers that Clorox didn't stand just for bleach but could also stand for detergents. This campaign failed miserably, and Clorox retreated from the market. When Miller Brewing Company introduced Miller Lite and Miller Genuine Draft Beers, its Miller High Life got lost in the shuffle. Miller High Life moved from a 23-million-barrel-a-year product and a strong number two behind Budweiser to a 6.4-million-barrel-a-year beer. What was once Miller's core beer, rather than being enhanced by flanker brand offshoots, was submerged by them.[4]

Brand impact is also greatly affected by innovation. Gillette's preeminent position in razors has been sustained not just by strong, pervasive advertising but also by brand enhancements such as the Sensor brand razor, a huge worldwide success. Putting more impact in a brand's offering may involve boosting the product's value in other ways. For instance, Chrysler's minivans were boosted in value as a family transportation choice when its models were offered with air conditioning and automatic transmission combined with a low base price, while other competitors sold these as optional extras.

In summary, when it comes to having creative impact, the keys are to ensure that the brand's point of difference is important to the target market (such as reliable appliances or safer tires) and then to convey this with consistent messages that bring the point home memorably. Memorable commercials in which the product's identity gets lost in the production values and from which customers can't recall *why* they should buy the brand are useless. Similarly, superbly differentiated products conveyed in consistently dull, lackluster advertising are just as big a loss. Powerful advertising is a little like the herring gull whose silver-gray plumage makes it blend into the sky, able to dive for fish in the ocean without being seen by its prey, yet conspicuous enough to attract other herring gulls (they can detect each other) when an abundance of food appears. Agencies want ads to be attention-getting (conspicuous) but not to overpower the product advertised (ad production values should be inconspicuous).

A brand is a complex amalgam of traits conveyed by its package, its price, its features, its color, and its copy line. Chivas Regal as a brand is not just an expression of one element; all must work in concert to convey prestige in a whiskey—or any other product. The Nike symbol, for instance, flows naturally on its shoe designs, and over onto ads along with the dramatic JUST DO IT theme line. So advertising must see that these elements work in concert, using sound, pictures, copy, music, and all sorts of sensory appeals to heighten the total effect. When all is said and done, however, the brand should have a clear point of difference from its competitors and be attractively positioned in this light in ads that neither detract from the positioning via overorchestration nor subdue the positioning through understatement.

Media Selection Efficiency

The process variable that counts most in media selection is efficiency, as shown in Figure 2-2. An efficient persuasion medium carries a message to its intended audience with as little waste as possible. Waste occurs when the message hits indifferent prospective buyers or buying influences. And the different media vary substantially in terms of their specificity and targeting possibilities.

Some media are inherently wasteful, but, because of their high-impact characteristics, are used anyway. Network television is an example of this. It costs huge amounts of money to produce and air television commercials on this medium, which has a mass targeting ability. Yet few products are truly mass products. Not everyone watching TV will be interested in buying the products most often advertised on it. For instance, children don't buy cars, yet the prime medium for automobile advertising is network television, which is also watched by these nondrivers. Computer companies such as Apple and IBM spend heavily on network television to advertise their hardware, yet many millions of viewers have zero interest in ever buying or using a computer. So television is a high-impact, low-specificity medium—in other words, a blunt instrument.

The best rule in media selection is to try and find the most specialized medium possible to deliver the message so as to minimize this waste factor. Narrow-spectrum specialized magazines hit more specific readers than newspapers do. MTV hits a specific target market of teenagers with less waste than network television does. Direct mail may be less wasteful than print ads are to market specialized products. Trade shows may showcase products to industrial or commercial buyers better than trade journals do. Radio may be a more targeted medium on a local level by submarket segment than local television is.

As a way of minimizing waste in media choices, Samsonite advertised its new line of sports bags for young adults on MTV and in *Rolling Stone, Cosmopolitan,* and *Glamour* magazines. Traditionally, its luggage is advertised on prime-time television or in broad-spectrum magazines such as *People* or *Fortune.* The demand for less wasteful media has resulted in new media being developed that offer very targeted messaging possibilities.

For example, Turner Broadcasting has developed an Airport Channel for specific ads to airport travelers. Whittle Communications has a TV medium that reaches into American schools.

Rick Adler has founded the Senior Network, a medium involving wallboards for advertising located inside seniors' community centers all across the United States, where the "over-fifty crowd" take fitness classes, Spanish courses, or just socializes two or three times a week. Adler's network includes 4,500 of America's largest centers, a great medium for advertisers of products whose target is people over fifty. (This group had a combined net worth in excess of $900 billion in the United States in 1991, and its discretionary income exceeds that of all other income groups.)

General Motors and Chrysler are even using direct mail to sell their cars. They send videocassettes of six to nine minutes' duration on new models, such as their vans, to U.S. households to more closely target potential buyers. Most of these tapes are sent to former buyers of their own vans or of competitors' vans in an effort to sell them on a new purchase. The tapes allow easy showcasing of the vans' new features and benefits.[5]

Media Buying Efficiencies

There are a variety of methods to boost media buying efficiencies quite apart from tighter targeting. These include buying media on a bundled basis from media groups that may own several stations in addition to selected magazines and newspapers. Discounts on specific placements may be available because of network "sell-offs" of space that has been undersubscribed. During the 1988 Olympics this became quite feasible on Canadian media television networks that were unable to sell all their available airtime surrounding every venue being broadcast during the two-week Winter Games held in Calgary that year. Olympic sponsors such as 3M bought as a package more spots than would normally have been available if airtime had been all presold. The network provided extra commercial insertions at minimal added cost to key sponsors in recognition of their overall customer importance to the network.

Airtime commercial positioning is becoming an increasingly important issue. Companies cannot gain the impact they desire on television if their commercials are aired at similar times to competitors' ads. A 1989 University of Cincinnati study demonstrated that when competitors' television commercials were aired too close together (say, during the same television show), brand-name recall decreased 25 percent and attribute/ad-claim recall fell 40 percent (versus scores when less competitive clutter exists). During some recent audits of television shows, as many as 40 to 50 percent of ads shown were for direct competitors. For instance, nine of eighteen spot commercials shown during an NBC prime-time show in the fall of 1991 were of competitors' products. One half-hour show, "Coach," featured two light-beer ads of rivals, three competitor automobile manufacturer ads, and two ads for feminine hygiene competitors.

To boost yield from media spending, companies must try much harder to avoid competitor head-to-head battles for viewers' attention during the same television show.

Figure 2-2 summarizes several media waste minimization tactics.

Promotion Efficiency

Promotions ought always to reinforce advertising because both convey a brand's identity. For example, Pillsbury's baking contests are a fine reinforcer of its brands, as are American Express's leather luggage tags, which reinforce the American Express image of status and prestige inherent in its membership credit card. So while promotional efficiency is critical, it must be tempered by the proviso that the promotion be compatible with the brand's point-of-difference. For instance, Nike markets its shoes on the basis of performance. If it continually promoted its shoes by means of

Figure 2-2 Media waste minimization.

- Buy bundled deals or sell-offs
- Avoid competitor clutter
- Niche where possible for high specificity by selecting
  - Regional vs. national media
  - Direct mail vs. print
  - Trade shows vs. journals
  - Specialty magazines vs. general print media
  - New networks, such as MTV, senior channels, Whittle in schools
  - Videocassettes to home
- Coordinate with PR, promotions
- Piggybacking on events

price-off deals or coupons, it would cheapen the performance message. However, a Nike promotion that used a consumer contest trip to an important sports event where performance is the highlight, such as the Olympics, a World Cup Soccer match, or World Track and Field Championships, would be quite compatible with Nike's ad image and product positioning.

Promotions can be contrasted as to their costs versus impacts. One key issue looks at selecting a promotional vehicle that combines the two variables of cost and impact for the greatest efficiency. For instance, product samples are an expensive, high-cost undertaking, but as a promotion vehicle sampling has high impact. Thus, high costs are offset by high impact (impact as measured by customers buying the product after the sample is gone because they tried and liked it). The spray lubricant WD-40 became a giant brand because it was extensively sampled, and the same is true of Armourall cleaner. Haagen Dazs superpremium ice cream has grown to more than a $100-million brand in Europe as a direct result of sampling promotions in key European cities. Normally 10 to 15 percent of customers who receive a free sample of a product subsequently buy it in the full-sized form. Contrast this efficiency with couponing, where only 2.5 percent of coupons are redeemed as a percentage of the dollars offered by couponers. Coupons are low in cost, but they are also very low in impact.

Excessive price promotions or "free goods" dealing to trade channel buyers, although they boost sales volume in the short run, do not boost sales or profits incrementally for any lasting effect on brand loyalty.[6] In fact, they teach consumers to wait for price breaks and teach the trade to do forward buying; that is, the trade stocks up on the promoted item at the tail end of the designated promotion period. In this way, the trade becomes plugged with the promoted lower-priced product, leaving less room in inventory for reorders at the higher regular price. This price promotion phenomenon has occurred not only in retail packaged goods. Autos and appliances that sell well with factory rebates also suffer big drops after the rebate promotion so that the net total sales effect is not incrementally any better.

Cross-promotions are a very fertile area of promotion because yields (eventual sales of product after the promotion) are often high while costs are medium since the co-promoters share the costs of advertising the promotion and the out-of-pocket charges for cross-couponing, cross-sampling, or joint pack-ins. For instance, Kellogg cross-promoted Lego building blocks in its children's cereals by using coupons on the package plus a small sample inside. Lego systems would have shared the promotion costs with Kellogg by providing product for the package insert at a very low cost, since Lego gains follow-along sales. Kellogg, for its part, gets the benefit of a popular children's item to help it sell more cereal than its rivals do. Cross-promotions are very efficient in terms of their cost/impact trade-offs.

Contests and sweepstakes can be very efficient promotional vehicles if contest participation levels are high, which is often a function of the creativity of the promotion itself. For instance, when General Foods gives away prizes for the best new Jell-O recipes, entries often number in the millions. When Osh Kosh B'Gosh, the apparel company, ran a contest for the best photo of a child in its clothing, it received 130,000 photo entries from all across America. Its sales were strongly boosted as customers bought their children Osh Kosh bib overalls for the entry photos.

Figure 2-3 illustrates graphically the concept of promotion vehicle efficiency trade-off.

In some instances, of course, the best promotion of a service is a money-back guarantee. Doctor's Hospital in Detroit promoted such a guarantee for its emergency ward services. If an emergency room patient waits longer than twenty minutes for service, it is provided free. This promotion was advertised on local cable television, and within six months emergency room business had climbed 30 percent. This is a very high-yield promotion, one that boosted both customer volume (revenue) and the hospital's overall reputation.

Other Cost-Saving Methods in Advertising/Promotion

To improve the yield of advertising or promotion isn't the only way to boost persuasion efficiency. A company can also maintain yield but cut costs. Here are several methods that are worth looking at.

1. *Tie ad agency commissions to campaign success rates.* For instance, Vons, California's largest grocer, offers its ad agency a

Figure 2-3. Promotion vehicles: How to diagnose/plot trade-offs.

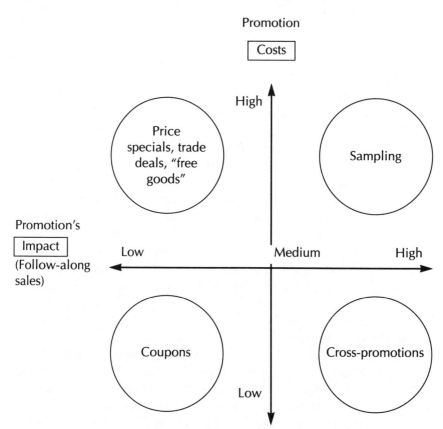

sliding-scale commission rate (from 7.5 percent to 25 percent) depending on whether customer traffic and sales of specifically advertised products soar during promotion periods. The traditional agency flat rate of 15 percent is being abandoned in favor of a performance-based *lower* base rate that moves higher as customer traffic exceeds 5 percent growth over the pre-advertising level.

2. *Standardize on a creative campaign for a large region.* IBM has done this for its PS/1 ads in Europe, where the company formerly developed different country-by-country ads. IBM saved $2 million in creative/production costs in 1990 by this standardization.[7] Leo Burnett created commercials for Kellogg's Frosted

Flakes that were able to be shown in twenty-two different countries around the globe. Coca-Cola launched identical television ads in 1992 for its four best-selling beverages in one hundred nations.

3. *Combine individual product ads and cross-merchandise families of products using common ad formats.* DuPont is doing this with its sleep products—pillows, mattress pads, mattress toppers, comforters, linens, and domestics. DuPont developed an ad campaign that included point-of-sale retail signing, brochures, posters, and informational displays, all of which were applicable across its diverse lines. DuPont sells a total sleep system using common ads, avoiding separate ads by product and all the accompanying signs and counter displays that each of these would entail.

4. *Use public relations (free publicity) to hold down costs.* Ateeco, the manufacturer of Mrs. T's pierogies, sponsors triathlons and biathlons, billing its product as the "official pierogi" of events such as the Chicago Marathon. The company sponsors more than 130 events at very low cost, but the publicity value is great in that Mrs. T's brand becomes well known and pierogies receive recognition for their healthful levels of carbohydrates—vitally necessary for triathletes in major competitions.[8]

5. *Try to trigger word-of-mouth advertising.* As an example, Magellan Systems of West Covina, California, increased sales of its handheld locational receivers from a million-dollar-per-year business in 1989 to $7.3 million in 1990 to $23 million in 1991, all via inexpensive word-of-mouth advertising. (These handheld receivers pinpoint a person's exact location on earth by using radio signals from orbiting satellites.) Magellan gave away 100 of its units (at a cost of $800 per unit) to high-profile, talkative adventurers and explorers (including a treasure hunter looking for Columbus's ships, a biologist tracking Arizona land tortoises, a Grand Canyon mapper, and an explorer crossing the Atlantic in a solar-powered boat). These people wrote or spoke about how useful the NAV 1000 device was to their unique challenges, and as a result more "ordinary" unit sales were made to boaters, hikers, oil and gas explorers, miners, and the military.[9]

6. *Recycle creative ideas that can still work.* A&W brands conjured up a very high-impact, low-cost television ad campaign by featuring in its commercials established characters from other

shows or commercials. For instance, it produced three television spots featuring: (1) Mr. Whipple, of Procter & Gamble's PLEASE DON'T SQUEEZE THE CHARMIN campaign, squeezing an A&W root beer can; (2) Madge, the manicurist of Palmolive dishwashing liquid fame, sticking her fingers in the A&W root beer; and (3) Mr. T of the "A-Team," finding that his gold jewelry chains keep falling into his mug of A&W root beer. By piggybacking on well-known personalities and commercials, A&W saved considerably on its campaign's creative costs. Both RCA and Old Spice (a Procter & Gamble brand) have also saved a lot in creative costs by recycling "old" creative material. RCA has resurrected Nipper the dog from bygone days, while Old Spice has brought back the whistling mariner from its 1960s commercials.

7. *Consolidate all agency work in the hands of fewer agencies.* In order to boost yield from agency spending, Procter & Gamble in 1992 consolidated its business from seven to two agencies-of-record only, hoping for greater clout from its consolidated budgets. Fewer agencies can prove to be tougher negotiators in syndicate media buying or network television when acting for a mega-client such as Procter & Gamble, which annually spends in excess of $750 million on media ads.

8. *Use the most precise methods to disseminate samples or coupons.* Precise sampling or couponing to a specific target group can be difficult via such mass media as newspapers or mass sample drops to the home. One method that holds promise as a less wasteful couponing or sampling technique is a program being run at movie theaters. General Cinema, in conjunction with Langworth Taylor, a promotions specialist, is sampling or couponing to movie theater patrons. This is very appealing as a low-waste, high-precision method because the product sampled or couponed can be tailored to the desired movie theater audience profile. Potential customers can be segmented by the age or sex of the likely moviegoer, depending on the film shown, the time of the film's showing, and even the theater location within a city. And theater patron sampling or couponing occurs without the competitive clutter that usually accompanies other sampling or couponing techniques. General Cinema is offering this service in 350 of its theaters and

has had an excellent reception from customers sampled and companies doing the sampling, such as Pepsico.

9. *Make creative materials modular so that when they are developed they can serve multiple purposes.* For instance, a print ad's creative can double as a point-of-sale poster for a store, or as a direct-mail stuffer for a distributor's mailing, or even as a leave-behind handout for sales reps making customer calls. The audio designed for airing with a television commercial can be created so that it can also be used directly as a radio commercial.[10]

10. *Lock in repeat customers with frequent-buyer promos to save advertising dollars spent on acquiring new customers.* As an example, Videoland, an Indiana chain of six stores, launched a "couch potato" promotion. Each time one of its members comes in, he or she receives a new, small gift—which continue through thirty-six rentals. For instance, gift #1 is a pop-top popper, gift #6 a chip clip, #12 a popcorn bowl, #18 an inflatable pillow, and #36 a blanket. This promotion encouraged repeat rentals during the winter months and rewarded regular customers for being couch potatoes. The promotion turned out to be a huge success and it cost Videoland very little in advertising, since it involved mostly in-store signage, posters, and a small ad in its video guide newsletter.

Figure 2-4 summarizes the various creative yield techniques discussed.

Figure 2-4. Creative yield methods.

- ○ Recycling (RCA, Timex, Old Spice)
- ○ Extensions
- ○ Families vs. one-up brands (cross-selling)
- ○ Consistency in theming (Maytag, Michelin, Heinz, Fed Ex)
- ○ Cross-promotions
- ○ Variable commissions with agencies
- ○ Corporation-identity policy—coordinate all its various facets, including print, electronic, point of sale, and packaging graphic images
- ○ Modularity of creative work for use in multiple media

Integrating Ads and Promotions for a Blended Effect

The yield from spending on ads and promotions will be much higher when spending is integrated between these for total brand impact. For instance, Guiness PLC of England spends about $7 million annually on advertising and promotion of its Johnny Walker Red brand Scotch whiskey. Half of this goes for ads in magazines, newspapers, billboards, phone kiosks, bus shelters, and commuter train posters, while the other half is spent on promotions or public relations aimed at both the trade and the public. These include six basic types of public relations or promotions, all working to reinforce the brand's imagery in ads:

1. *Bar/restaurant merchandisers*, such as bottle stands, table tents, bar mats, mirrors, and napkin holders
2. *Product placements on television shows and in motion pictures*
3. *In-store liquor store/grocery store displays* for special occasions such as Christmas or Father's Day
4. *Sponsorships of sporting events*, such as World Championship Golf or professional horse show jumping
5. *Special packaging*, such as holiday gift packs, year-round gift cartons
6. *Distributor promotions*, such as sales incentive contests for the Johnny Walker distributor sales force

The resulting brand impact has created a $175 million business for Johnny Walker Red, since all the ad, promo, and public relations bases are well covered. Dr. Ken Hardy, in his landmark study of successful versus unsuccessful promotions, showed how promotions that are advertised yield considerably better results than those not advertised. This validated the multiplier effect of integrating ads and promos to obtain maximum effect.[11]

Measuring System Yield

Regardless of the promotion or ad medium used, measurement of the impact is crucial. The four items most commonly measured are:

1. *Leads generated*—from journal ads, direct mailers, trade shows, 800-number call-ins, and so on
2. *Redemption rates*—for coupons or sweepstakes contest entries
3. *Participation rates*—in contests or in incentive campaigns by distributors, dealers, or retailers, or at trade shows as measured by booth traffic
4. *Ad recall and recognition scores*—of brand awareness, attributes, and images from television or radio commercials, print ads, billboard campaigns, or event sponsorships

Each of these provides some concrete measure of the impact of persuasion spending, apart from sales growth, which is usually affected by the total marketing system of the company, and not by the persuasion system component *alone*.

Certification of Advertising, Public Relations, and Promotion Agencies

Consistent with any continuous-improvement culture, a company ought to demand that its appointed agencies, to whom it delegates persuasion system work, be in tune with a total quality management approach. This requires that, as suppliers, these agencies demonstrate a commitment to TQM principles and practices. This can occur in three visible ways:

1. *Demonstrated commitment of the agency's chief executives to total quality management principles*, that is, to programs for continuous improvement in the agency's own operations, service, and personnel practices. The agency can be graded on how prepared it is to take action on client problems or to join in quality audits when desired by the client.

2. *Benchmarked and constantly measured performance in quality areas the agency impacts*. For instance, the agency's work can be measured by its timeliness (whether it meets deadlines); unit costs (whether it adheres to the budgets established); cycle time improvements (the length of time it takes to turn around a job from start to finish); error rates in invoicing or agency paper-

Figure 2-5. Major process improvement strategies in marketing persuasion systems.

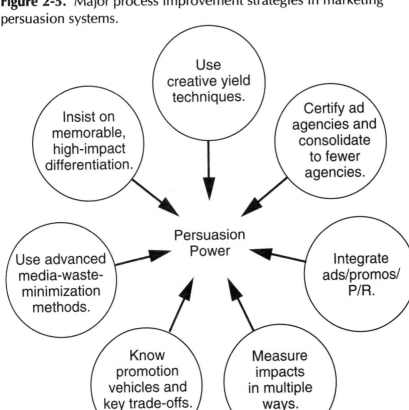

work systems; amounts of rework owing to agency-induced errors; compliance of the work with client specifications/guidelines; and the appearance and completeness of the work it does.

3. *The agency's skills in customer handling, communication, use of technology, and creativity.* These would include how the agency handles customers during complaint sessions, emergencies, or tight deadlines; how skillful the agency's presentations are and how well it communicates in meetings or via telephone, fax, and written communications; the agency's level of technology in graphic design equipment (such as desktop publishing); and the

agency's creative ability to generate new ideas and come up with winning campaigns.

All these practices, so common with vendor certifications in manufacturing, should be adopted by agencies along with continuous-improvement concepts. Agencies can be first-rate at producing work that is nice to look at and to show, but if they underperform on time responsiveness, budget discipline, communications, paperwork flow, or transactional accuracy, it's difficult ever to get total quality into a company's persuasion system management.

Figure 2-5 summarizes the seven key strategies for process improvement in persuasion systems.

Notes

1. Julie Liesse, "Brands in Trouble," *Advertising Age* (December 2, 1991), pp. 16, 18, 50.
2. *Ibid.*, p. 18.
3. C. Power, "Value Marketing," *Business Week* (November 11, 1991), pp. 132–138.
4. M. Landler, Z. Schiller, and L. Therrien, "What's in a Name?" *Business Week* (July 8, 1991), pp. 66, 67.
5. R. Serafin, "Mini Van Battle Carried to Videocassettes," *Advertising Age* (July 1, 1991), p. 12.
6. K. Hammond and A. S. C. Ehrenberg, "The After Effects of Consumer Promotions," *London Business School Report* (August 1991).
7. "IBM Uses Identical Ads for Europe," *The Wall Street Journal* (April 16, 1991), p. B7.
8. Matthew Grimm, "Mrs. T's Pierogies—Sports Endurance Brand," *Marketing Week* (July 15, 1991), p. 15.
9. "Do-It-Yourself Marketing," *Inc.* magazine (November 1991), pp. 55, 56.
10. Richard Gibson, "Marketer's Mantra: Reap More With Less," *The Wall Street Journal* (March 22, 1991), p. B2.
11. Dr. Kenneth Hardy, "Key Success Factors for Manufacturers' Sales Promotions in Packaged Goods," *The Journal of Marketing* 50 (July 1986), pp. 13–23.

3

The Selling System

*It's no trick to be a successful salesman, if you have what
the people want. You never hear the bootleggers complaining
about hard times.*

Bob Edwards
1922

A selling system is one of the more complex systems in marketing.
It involves not only all the components of sales-representative effectiveness but also the components of sales force management
and administration. So looking for process improvement—that is,
lower waste, greater yield, better time responsiveness, increased
proficiency, or higher capacity—can mean both searching that
part of the selling system that is under the sales rep's control and
examining the larger sales management part of the system involving rep recruitment, deployment, supervision, compensation, and
appraisal. Figure 3-1 examines both these functions of the system.

The effectiveness of either part of the system is moderated by
the age and experience level of the reps and the sales managers,
as well as by the tenor of the competition. When competition is
fierce or cutthroat, it presents much tougher effectiveness challenges than when it is more moderate and predictable. Performing
under high stress stretches the capacities and capabilities of systems considerably. Seasoned sales professionals, whether managers or reps, can usually handle more pressure than a more junior,
less seasoned crew of reps or managers.

Figure 3-1. The selling system's two main components and their functions.

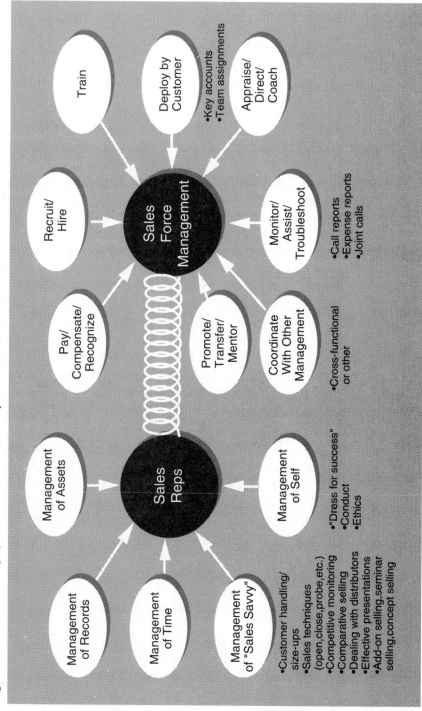

Why Quality Improvement Is Critical

Diagnosing a selling system using process variables to boost the system's yield or response time is critical for a variety of reasons.

○ Selling systems are costly; in fact, they are one of marketing's most costly processes. Large sales forces are expensive. They cost a great deal to recruit and train, to equip with sales aids and tools, to incentivize with pay plans and other motivators, to reimburse for travel to accounts, and to provide with cars, cellular phones, expense accounts, and laptop computers. And some sales force costs continue to escalate almost without abatement, such as airline costs, meal costs, gasoline costs, auto repair or insurance fleet costs, entertaining costs (for customers), hotel costs, and costs of rep hardware such as laptop computers and software. Some of these costs, such as salaries or equipment depreciation, are fixed, not variable with sales revenues. So, given the level of spending in this area, finding ways to use process analysis to increase sales force efficiency can have dramatic paybacks.

○ The selling system often epitomizes the company in the eyes of the end customer or distributor. Thus, improvements in response time, yield, or proficiency pay off in a better reputation for the company as a whole.

○ The selling system is one of the most flexible of marketing's systems. Sales reps can literally customize their approaches, product offerings, and services to the level of specific accounts. So selling systems can be a great source of competitive advantage given their inherent flexibility to customize. For instance, pharmaceutical sales reps customize their presentations by physician call to take into account the doctor's specific clinical practice and current drug of referral. Fine-tuning other marketing systems, such as the persuasion system (advertising, public relations, promotion) or the product innovation system, to meet individual customer needs is much more difficult.

○ Selling-system yield can be dramatically affected by rep turnover in a territory, by account defections, or by distributor conflict, all of which take place at the field level. So system vulnerability is very high in selling. This makes it all the more imperative to constantly improve the yields, responsiveness, efficiency, and capacity of both reps and managers.

o As target customers of the seller qualify and certify fewer key vendors (with whom they will deal), pushing for selling-system improvements becomes a necessity, or the selling company may find itself on the outside looking in, having lost out on the vendor short list to a competitor who demonstrates higher total quality in its selling and value-added services.

o The selling system is more amenable to measurement than is any other subsystem of marketing. It is quite possible to measure yields per territory, and per person, and to get a handle on time wasters, money wasters, or other activity inefficiencies. The proficiency of reps can often be tested and measured through observation. The responsiveness to customer complaints can be measured, as can the cycle time it takes to get back to customers regarding queries received or requests for sales calls or literature. Sales lead follow-up monitoring can help gauge cycle time on lead fulfillment. Thus, selling-system process improvements, as they are implemented, can usually be measured to see whether the new initiatives are working to good effect. It is tougher to ferret out waste or other system outputs when looking at advertising, where measurements are frequently inexact or missing entirely.

Key Process Variables

The key process variables worth examining in a selling system are those that have the greatest effect on sales, costs, or customer satisfaction. Customers care greatly about a sales force's responsiveness to their needs and the capacity of the company to cover their demands for instruction in the product's use, benefits, and productivity effects. So customer satisfaction would mandate looking at:

- o Selling-system responsiveness
- o Selling-system capacity (to cover accounts)
- o Selling-system proficiency (to assist in customer product training and problem solving)

Leveraging costs lower while achieving sales growth targets would necessitate focusing on areas of spending waste in the system. In addition, a selling system's complexity might need to be studied to determine if simplification in management procedures, paperwork controls, and pay plans could cut costs. The selling system's flexibility to accommodate changing circumstances, such as shifting customer preferences, distributor needs, or competitors, is also worth looking at for leveraging revenues over time. Yields per account, per region, or per rep are worth examining for clues as to their improvement.

Because specializing a sales force increases costs owing to the costs of higher training and having more qualified reps in the system, a selling system aiming at greater efficiency must consider both the cost side of specialization and the higher average sales results that usually flow from fielding better, more specialized personnel. So system efficiency can be gauged on two dimensions: sales cost effects and sales revenue effects.

Figure 3-2 summarizes how various process dynamics can be applied to improve customer satisfaction and to increase sales rev-

Figure 3-2. Process variables worth studying to improve a selling

Process Variable	Key Sales Dynamic Being Improved
1. Capacity 2. Responsiveness 3. Proficiency	Improve customer satisfaction.
4. Waste 5. Complexity	Cut sales force costs.
6. Yield 7. Flexibility	Grow sales revenues.
8. Efficiency $\longrightarrow$	Grow $\uparrow$ sales revenues (outputs) by more than changes in costs (inputs).

enues while cutting or containing sales costs. In other words, process variables can be analyzed as to their effect on the total quality effort by sales reps.

Improving Quality in the Sales Rep's Activities

Areas in which the sales rep can aim for improvement include better management of the self, of assets, of records, of sales savvy, and of time.

Management of Self

The quality of a sales rep's efforts can be improved by focusing on two process dynamics here, namely rep capacity and flexibility. The key to increasing a rep's capacity to sell and more flexibly handle different selling situations, customer types, or products is by way of training courses or individual study. The rep's capacity to sell is boosted because training cuts the learning-curve time before full rep productivity is reached. The rep's flexibility is boosted as he or she learns to routinize approaches to quite different customers with far less scrambling and far more confidence.

Management of Assets

As reps become skilled in the productive use of such technology as car phones and laptops and such routine working tools as samples, presentation kits, and their own briefcases and cars, their efficiency is boosted considerably. They are able to prepare better for calls through practicing their presentations and organizing their appointments more effectively, as well as to handle emergency calls more efficiently through the increased contact with customers made possible by cellular phones. If the software used with the laptop allows the rep to prepare on-the-spot customer selling proposals (or to revise these), considerable efficiency results since the rep need not arrange to have these typed or mailed separately to the accounts after qualifying each account's needs on the sales call. In addition, laptops' graphic capabilities allow reps to make much more polished proposals to customers. Hewlett-Packard found that it could cut the time its reps spent in meetings from 13 percent to 7 percent (a 50 percent improvement) by communicating with its reps electronically.

Management of Records

A sales rep who maintains excellent account records, profiling key data about customer purchases (when and how much was bought), key influencers and contacts, and buying concerns or obstacles, can substantially increase his or her proficiency. This is because the rep's records provide the key information needed for call sequence timing and pre-call preparation. In effect, the records provide clues as to when a call will be most welcome and what the customers' "hot buttons" are relative to their needs. If such records are well maintained, the complexity of selling is greatly simplified because updates to records can double as call reports to the sales manager. And when a new rep is assigned the territory, the start-up handoff is made smoother by the existence of complete and up-to-date account records.

Gaining Sales "Savvy"

Sales rep savvy can be broken down into four components: heightened responsiveness, greater proficiency, more efficiency, and increased yield. The ability to respond can be improved by means of team selling in which the rep works with other teammates to more effectively assist customers. Computer companies often do this by teaming sales reps with systems analysts who then jointly call on accounts and have a greater capability of addressing all the account's concerns about a computer installation or sale (from pricing, terms, and features to technical software questions or concerns about training, repair service, and so on). Proficiency in sales rep savvy could mean reps learning to upsell customers by augmenting the basic sale of an item with possible add-ons. Furniture salespeople do this when they sell the basics (a couch, chair, or suite) and then upgrade the sale with accessories (lamps, artwork, decorative accents, a small rug). Even farm dealer salespeople do this when they upsell a combine to include such extras as an air-conditioned cab, a stereo, or more comfortable seats.

An efficiency focus in the area of sales savvy could look at ways to sell customers in groups rather than one by one. This technique, called seminar selling, is used extensively with professionals such as doctors, nurses, architects, or engineers who attend seminars to upgrade their education and in the process are exposed to new products/systems. Health-care manufacturers who sell their products to groups of nurses often employ this technique. Yield improvements from sales savvy often require the greater use of teleselling, since teleselling personnel can supplement face-to-face visits by field reps and qualify sales leads with greater productivity. Skandia Insurance uses its DIAL telemarketing unit to sell basic life insurance in Denmark, Norway, and Sweden. This lower-cost sales technique allows Skandia to sell policies for 30 percent lower than competing policies sell for.[1] 3M uses telesales personnel to cover small hospitals or clinics ordering medical products such as tapes, masks, electrodes, surgical incise drapes, and other products made by 3M.

Management of Time

How sales reps manage their time greatly affects waste in selling and the amount of time they can spend with customers. A great many hours of precious sales time can be eaten up by nonsales activities such as meetings and paperwork, so if effective management of nonsales activities can be achieved less waste will result. Because a rep's capacity to make sales is greatly affected by even small increases in "face-time" spent with customers, control of nonsales tasks usually boosts order volume and new account prospecting. Time management training courses for reps as well as cellular phones and computers help achieve these goals of more face-to-face sales time and less waste in a rep's routines. Cellular phones allow a rep to use otherwise unproductive time on the road to set up customer appointments, to follow up on or expedite problem orders, and to orchestrate inside staff at his or her own company to assist customers in whatever way they desire (by providing technical advice, arranging shipping, sorting out credit issues, handling complaints, answering questions about warranties, and so forth). Computers with preformatted software can be used in customers' offices for on-the-spot price quotes and competitor offer comparisons displayed on the screen side by side against the company's offer. Figure 3-3 relates rep activities discussed previously to the process variable impacted by such activities.

Total Quality in Sales Force Management

Figure 3-1 outlines the elements that sales managers use to effect changes in rep behavior—and ultimately sales results. Such elements include recruitment, hiring, training, deployment, compensation, supervision, appraisal, advancement, or transfers. Sales managers juggle these demands on their skills and time in molding a high-sales-effectiveness-oriented team. From a system stand-

Figure 3-3. How sales rep activities affect key sales process variables.

Sales Process Variable / Target Improvement Area	Sales Rep Activities				
	Management of Self	Management of Assets	Management of Records	Sales "Savvy"	Management of Time
Capacity	✓				✓
Responsiveness				✓	
Proficiency			✓	✓	
Waste					✓
Complexity			✓		
Yield				✓	
Flexibility	✓				
Efficiency		✓		✓	

point, each of these elements affects different process variables and outcomes.

For instance, the recruitment criteria used by a sales manager may ultimately determine the intellectual capacity of a rep to handle complex product selling, concept selling, or senior-management-level contacts in target customer companies. Because IBM sells complex systems and computing solutions and these are often big-ticket purchases, it always recruits and hires sales reps with advanced college degrees. Many chemical companies hire engineers as their sales reps, because they consider it more efficient to teach an engineer selling skills than to try and teach a first-class sales rep without an engineering degree all about engineering. Chemical sales reps usually sell to buyers or specifiers who are themselves engineers. 3M sells its hospital laser imagers to X-ray departments using former radiology technicians it has trained to be salespeople.

Training for the Greatest Impact

Rep capacity is also greatly affected by training. For example, Merck, the pharmaceutical giant, invests heavily in training its reps so as to enhance their credibility with physicians and pharmacists. Merck provides training in the basics of medicine, including anatomy, physiology, and pathology. Merck then spends months training reps in the properties and side effects of all the drugs they will detail to doctors, as well as in the properties of their competitors' products. Reps get training updates on the basic research into diseases that their drugs are used to treat and are given any research or clinical studies outlining the efficacy of Merck's versus competitors' drugs by disease treated.[2] Training of course affects reps' capacities in quite varied ways. In Merck's case, it affects their sales capacity with prescribing physicians.

Cooper Tire teaches its reps how to handle tire dealers' needs and concerns and to deal with dealers in the dealers' own jargon. Cooper teaches reps to understand how Cooper's dealers do their merchandising, put together their tire displays and their advertising, and indeed even how a dealer's cash flow, balance sheet, inventory position, and return on investment are managed.

How a sales manager deploys reps—by account or territory or

vertical market—has a big impact on sales yield. Through the manager's direction and assignments, yield can be maximized on the basis of the volume potential of different geographic zones, different industries, or, specifically, certain key accounts. If Pareto's Law (the 80/20 rule) operates, yield by market or account or territory can be greatly leveraged so long as the manager deploys reps against those accounts "where 80 percent of the action is." Selling harder or smarter doesn't bring much net gain if such efforts fail to hit the largest potential accounts, biggest vertical markets, or most important geographic pockets of demand.

Two examples illustrate the power of deployment to boost yield. Apple Computer dominates the desktop publishing market in part because it has specialized its sales force to know and canvass this market more aggressively than its competitors do.

H. B. Fuller, a manufacturer of more than a thousand different adhesives, sells to more than a hundred different industries. When it decided to redeploy its reps from covering broad territories with all products to specializing in selected products to vertical markets (containing the biggest adhesive users), H. B. Fuller doubled its sales in five years. Its reps became experts in high-consuming, adhesive-using industries such as bookbinding/publishing and, as such, became consultants to their customers. 3M has specialized key account reps who handle aerospace customers for a variety of 3M products. These large customers, such as Boeing or McDonnell Douglas, by getting more focused attention from 3M, have provided 3M with far more growth than a less specialized deployment would have yielded. Aerospace customers have actually had 3M invent special products just for them.

When a sales manager sets up teams to handle customers, the benefits usually include not only higher yield but also more rapid responsiveness. For instance, teaming a manufacturer's rep with a distributor's rep to make joint customer calls can ensure that the customer gets more of a "total sale," including the product expertise of the factory rep and the service expertise and follow-up of the distributor rep, who ultimately writes the order. Rep teams can take many variations. Reps can team with customer service or with technical personnel for better, faster account servicing. Reps may even team with factory production personnel if product customization is required to meet the customer's specific need. DuPont did this for large electronics customers who buy their electronic components. Since these are often customized, having production personnel on the call quickens the responsiveness of the factory to produce the custom componentry.

The efficiency and flexibility dimensions of sales management are most affected by decisions on rotational assignments. When reps are rotated between assignments, they wind up cross-trained on one another's accounts and territories. This can boost efficiency when turnover occurs in the sales ranks, and accounts of the departing rep need to be covered by the other cross-trained rep.

Waste Management

Lowering waste in that part of the selling system affected by managers involves two facets. First, managers can lower waste by using variable pay plans for rep performance. In this way, reps are incentivized to productive selling by their compensation. Usually this variable portion does not exceed 20–30 percent of their pay. A larger commission percentage often provides reps with too little incentive for finding new accounts or doing the long-term market development activities to bring along these accounts, which have an extended payoff but do not produce immediately commissionable new business.

Second, waste can be minimized by the sales manager acting as a traffic cop concerning the rest of the organization's demands on a rep's time. Managers may need actively to keep other members of the company from wasting the rep's time if such activities distract or pull the rep away from customers and the ability to provide excellent customer service. This rep "protection" may even extend to shielding reps from senior management figures, who may be keen to travel with the sales force from time to time, a situation that may or may not be viewed as positive by customers.

Coaching/Mentoring Sales Reps

One of the biggest system capacity improvements in sales is brought about by the manager mentoring a rep's development over time. A top-notch sales manager usually develops good people over the course of his or her management tenure. The systematic mentoring of a sales force requires a manager to sit down and sort the reps into performance categories. Some reps are fast-trackers, or superstars. Others are steady but average producers. Still others are only marginal producers who struggle constantly to hit their sales targets and to service their accounts. How the manager mentors or coaches the rep is a function of how such reps are categorized. The coaching or mentoring plan for superstar reps ought to be a maintenance action plan (MAP) designed to hold the reps' performance at high levels. The coaching/mentoring plan for the average, steady-producing sales reps ought to be a developmental action plan (DAP) designed to upgrade or boost sales results and proficiency. The coaching/mentoring plan for the subpar struggling-to-produce rep ought to be a remedial action plan (RAP) designed to improve performance quickly above the marginal level. (The alternative is to transfer such reps to different positions or to terminate them.) Figure 3-4 models the three plans.

There are of course numerous tools that can be used to upgrade a rep's performance (or to sustain it). These include new

Figure 3-4. Mentoring plans for sales rep development.

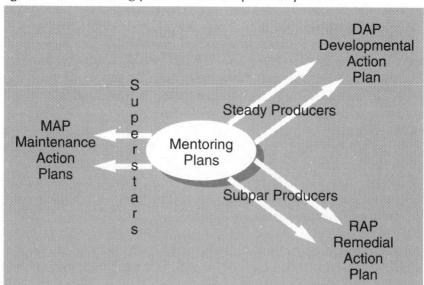

experiential assignments, further training, lateral transfers, outside company leadership roles (in service clubs, charities, sports organizations), or special in-company assignments (for instance, assigning a rep to train peer reps on a new product or to organize a regional sales meeting). One recent major study of those factors contributing to sales force effectiveness (conducted by the University of North Florida) demonstrated strong correlations between (1) strong training early in a rep's selling career and excellent sales performance and (2) assignments/coaching in which the rep learns to be a good "team player" (with other inside customer service personnel) and subsequent top sales performance.[3]

Figure 3-5 is a grid that shows the tools that a manager can draw on arrayed against rep performance categories. Clearly, which tools are applied depends on how the rep's performance is tracking.

INLAND STEEL: A LESSON IN APPLYING PROCESS IMPROVEMENT LOGIC TO A SELLING SYSTEM

Inland Steel Company is the fourth-largest steel manufacturer in the United States, producing $2.5 billion per year in revenues. This represents about 6 percent of the market. As part of Inland's total quality management emphasis, it undertook a major overhaul of its selling system to improve competitiveness. Inland sought to increase the yield of its sales force by redeploying reps from territories to key accounts. It sought to increase the capacity of its sales reps by specializing them by strategic industry cluster. And it sought to improve responsiveness/cycle time on customer demands by organizing the sales force into team units, headed by strategic account managers and empowered to enlist any Inland resources that were necessary to boost customer satisfaction. These strategic account managers can even call upon Inland's CEO to assist with key customers, because he is a member of several of these teams. To achieve this selling system transformation, Inland invested heavily in team building, training, and information systems that track strategic account purchases, deliveries, special needs, prices paid, and services offered.

The upshot of all of this? In 1982, Inland sold 3,000 customers

(*text continues on page 54*)

Figure 3-5. The components of sales rep mentoring.

Mentoring Tools \ Mentoring Categories	Fast Trackers	Steady, Solid Performers	Struggling to Produce
On-the-Job Challenges			
Courses/Night School, etc.			
Cross-Pollination (Transfer)			
Team Assignments (in area)			
Formal Performance Appraisals			
Leadership Assignments			
Advancement (into managment or senior "career" sales positions)			
Noncompany-Related Challenges (that develop leadership)			

Figure 3-6. Initiatives for total-quality sales force management.

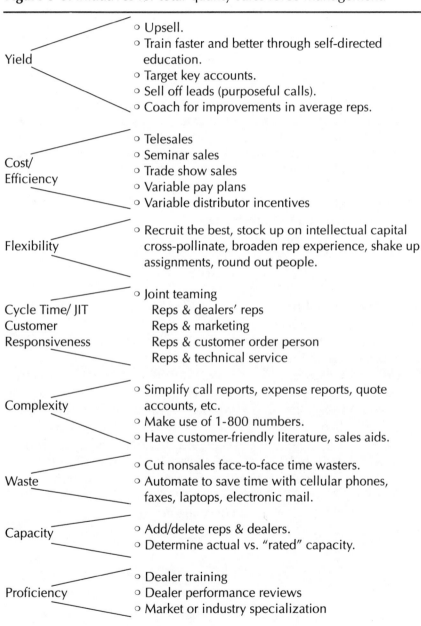

Yield
- Upsell.
- Train faster and better through self-directed education.
- Target key accounts.
- Sell off leads (purposeful calls).
- Coach for improvements in average reps.

Cost/ Efficiency
- Telesales
- Seminar sales
- Trade show sales
- Variable pay plans
- Variable distributor incentives

Flexibility
- Recruit the best, stock up on intellectual capital cross-pollinate, broaden rep experience, shake up assignments, round out people.

Cycle Time/ JIT Customer Responsiveness
- Joint teaming
  Reps & dealers' reps
  Reps & marketing
  Reps & customer order person
  Reps & technical service

Complexity
- Simplify call reports, expense reports, quote accounts, etc.
- Make use of 1-800 numbers.
- Have customer-friendly literature, sales aids.

Waste
- Cut nonsales face-to-face time wasters.
- Automate to save time with cellular phones, faxes, laptops, electronic mail.

Capacity
- Add/delete reps & dealers.
- Determine actual vs. "rated" capacity.

Proficiency
- Dealer training
- Dealer performance reviews
- Market or industry specialization

a total of $2.4 billion worth of steel. By 1990, Inland had cut its customer base by more than 90 percent to 200 strategic accounts. But the yield per account was greater than ever, since in 1990 Inland sold a total of $3.8 billion to these 200 accounts. Inland's approach to boosting yield and responsiveness in sales was merely part of a larger endeavor to turn the whole company's competitiveness upside down. Inland was also modernizing its manufacturing, cutting waste in administrative staffing, and improving its relations with the steelworkers' union. But its systematic use of process improvement principles vividly illustrates how both customer satisfaction and yield from a sales force can be leveraged using the mind-set of a systems engineer.[4]

Essential strategies for total quality in selling systems are briefly summarized in Figure 3-6.

Notes

1. "Skandia's Dial Insurance," *The Wall Street Journal* (March 16, 1991), p. 16.
2. Allan J. Magrath, *The Revolution in Sales and Marketing* (New York: AMACOM Books, 1990), pp. 123–124.
3. University of North Florida 1991 study of sales force effectiveness factors. Conducted for the National Paper Trades Association of America by Professor Adel El-Ansary. (Unpublished.)
4. Robert J. Darnall, "Inland Steel: From Competitive Gap to Competitive Advantage," speech before the 1990 Planning Forum, April 28–May 1, 1991, Toronto, contained in the 1990 *International Conference Executive Summary* (Oxford, Ohio: The Planning Forum, 1991), pp. 6–9. (Selected data on sales from Inland Industries' annual shareholders' report.)

4

The Incentivizing System

Too many crooks spoil the percentage.

H. Chandler

Inducing customers to purchase products or services involves setting base prices and discounts that will result in the highest possible yield in top-line revenues and bottom-line profits. System yield is the key output variable to focus on. Characteristics of price inducement systems that also count are the system's flexibility (to adjust over time to market shifts) and the system's complexity. The more complex an incentivizing system is, the greater the opportunities are for errors in invoicing, price quoting, tendering, and price negotiating to occur. Zero-defect pricing demands manageable simplicity in the price-setting system to avoid confusion and communication difficulties.

There is, of course, a wide range of inducements possible in an incentivizing system. Inducements can include discounts for early payment and low-cost financing (or extended terms) for purchases bought on credit. Inducements can be volume discounts based on the number of units bought or the absolute dollar size of orders placed. Such volume discounts can be paid out as earned, or they can be accumulated and paid as yearly rebates. The form of the discounts can also vary, from reductions in the invoiced price to the provision of free goods in lieu of an invoice price reduction. Some inducements may involve the seller forgoing costs in order to incentivize purchase, for example, by absorbing delivery freight costs, product installation costs, or after-sale product-training costs. On durable goods, trade-in allowances on an old product are often used to induce the sale of the new product.

Figure 4-1 models the three key elements of an incentivizing system and the three salient process variables worth improving.

The Risk Attached to Pricing Decisions

Of all the systems in marketing, pricing is one of the riskiest. This is because changes in price usually generate an almost immediate competitive reaction. In addition, prices in a great many markets may be subject to government scrutiny or control. For instance, utility rates are often regulated, some transportation costs may be

Figure 4-1. The incentivizing system and key process variables to improve.

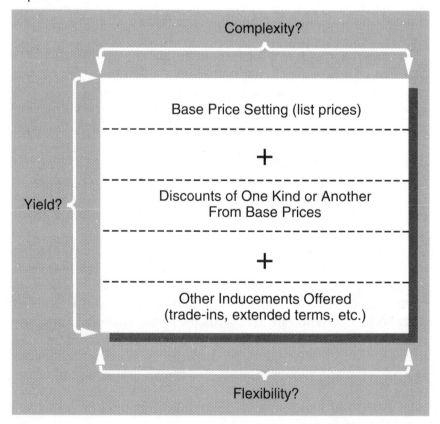

affected by government levies, and telecommunications rates and prescription drug prices in some nations are regulated. Pricing decisions are unique relative to other marketing systems inasmuch as they can be adjusted relatively quickly. Channel systems or product innovation systems may take months or even years to alter significantly, and even marketing persuasion systems and selling systems take significant periods of time to change. Prices, by contrast, can be changed very fast. For example, bank interest rates, which represent the price of borrowing, are often changed in a matter of minutes, and these changes are disseminated electronically around the world by money traders and wire services.

Boosting Yield in Pricing

Inducing customers to purchase at the highest possible prices consistent with market share targets requires an organization to maintain optimum competitiveness, manage costs effectively, customize prices by customer segment served, and keep brand equity and category clout as high as possible across all the products in the line. Figure 4-2 models these four factors.

Competitiveness

How good a deal a company offers customers is a trade-off between the price and the perceived value (benefits) the customer gets relative to what the competition offers. This can be graphed, as in Figure 4-3. Competitiveness, or competitive advantage, can only be gained if the trade-off between perceived value versus rivals and price moves farther out the utility line on this graph.

If a company drops prices but cuts benefits, or boosts benefits (value) while putting prices up, it is not enhancing its competitive position. It is merely repositioning its benefit/price trade-off. Improving the benefit/price trade-off means boosting benefits (value) while holding prices, dropping prices, or boosting prices only marginally while significantly improving benefits. Computer companies constantly try to alter their competitiveness by dropping prices while at the same time boosting their computer's capacity, processing speed, or features. This is represented by moving from

Figure 4-2. A pricing yield model.

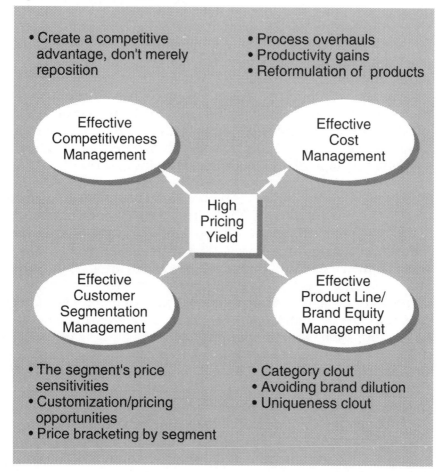

A to F on the graph. Automakers frequently move from A to C, improving their car's value or features (air bags, anti-lock braking, rust-proofing) while at the same time increasing price (moving along the price axis to the left). Because their stance usually doesn't confer competitive advantage on any one of them, they can become vulnerable to any rival who can boost features while holding prices down (moving from A to E). Attempts by car companies to give away options such as power steering or air conditioning at no extra cost are in some ways a variation on this A-to-E strategy.

Figure 4-3. Price competitiveness options.

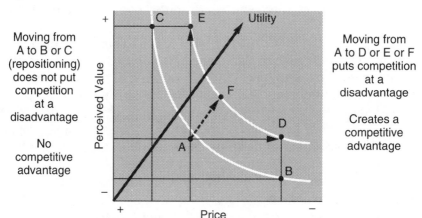

Moving from A to B or C (repositioning) does not put competition at a disadvantage

No competitive advantage

Moving from A to D or E or F puts competition at a disadvantage

Creates a competitive advantage

The introduction by Advanced Micro Devices of its 386 SX computer chip, with thirty-five megahertz power (versus Intel's lower twenty megahertz power), for the identical price as the Intel computer chip, gained 13 percent of the market for the new product in only two years. This is a classic A-to-E move, offering better value at the same price as competition.

When the Hyundai automobile (from South Korea) was first introduced in North America, it positioned itself moving from A to D, using aggressive price cuts while keeping its competitive features and value-added options equivalent to those of other low-cost and midrange foreign imports. Hyundai succeeded initially in gaining share because of this tactic, only to fall back later on when its product's "fit and finish" were judged by the market to be less than "Japanese quality standards" (especially in Canada, where its rust-proofing proved inferior when it failed to stand up to the road salt in winter).

Cost Management and Pricing

Giving customers a good trade-off between price and benefits doesn't mean a company can sustain this "good customer deal" if the costs of providing such benefits get out of line and company profits start eroding in the attempt to continue the deal. A vivid example illustrates this. Taco Bell decided to boost its sales by cutting prices on its most popular entrées in 1991. As a result, sales jumped 17 percent that year. But in order not to erode profits at the same time, Taco Bell had to manage its costs in a radically different and more productive way. It decided to get out of the food-preparation and cooking part of the restaurant business and instead assigned to its suppliers the task of delivering to it precooked, ready-to-assemble meat and vegetables for stuffing into prefried taco shells. This saved fifteen man-hours in labor per store per week. In addition, Taco Bell cut the number of its store supervisors by two-thirds to further lower its costs. Each of these moves has allowed Taco Bell to continue to offer enhanced price competitiveness without a loss in profits.[1] Astute price management requires astute cost management.

There are a number of cost-management techniques that can help a company to sustain a benefit/price trade-off that is considered the best around. One is to substitute lower-cost materials for key product components. Automakers have done this with plastics in place of rubber, among other substitutions. For instance, Ford is testing whether palladium, a cheaper alternative to expensive platinum, can be substituted in catalytic converters for its cars.

Outsourcing key components to more efficient vendors is another way to hold down costs and allow for competitive pricing. Timex used to make most of its watch parts itself, but decided to outsource these and use its scale-volume buying clout to reduce its watch-part costs. This had been very successful in allowing Timex to stay competitively priced despite the fast-paced and cut-throat nature of watch competition.[2]

Process redesign of manufacturing also can help a company to stay price-competitive. Integrated steel producers in America have lost ten share points since 1982 to minimill steelmakers such as Nucor and Chaparral Steel, which can underprice them because these minimills use more efficient processes and use scrap to make steel (versus making it from scratch as is done by integrated producers such as Allegheny Ludlum). Caterpillar's tractor-factory automation program has helped keep its unit costs of production competitive against the likes of Komatsu, a relentless low-cost producer of heavy machinery. Frito-Lay hopes to save $35 million per year in its snack food operations by automating its final process, filling shipping cartons with its bags of snacks, which currently is done manually because of the difficulty of doing this without crushing the snacks.

Eileen Shapiro, a well-known management consultant, focuses on the interplay among pricing, benefits, and costs in a conception she calls the Strategic Triangle.* All major decisions in a corporation in one way or another affect the benefits customers receive, the price paid for these, or the costs incurred to provide these benefits. The left side of the triangle, pictured in Figure 4-4, represents (in the customer's eyes) how good a deal the customer is receiving; the right side represents how profitable this can be, since the difference between price and cost is shown here; and the bottom part of the triangle represents the difficulty inherent in providing the benefits at costs that are sustainable. It is in the bottom part of the triangle that a company needs to use its ingenuity to lower its costs with product reformulation, factory or sales productivity improvements, or other cost-management techniques such as process redesign.

Effective Customer Segmentation for Pricing Yields

Although a company's costs effectively represent a floor in pricing (especially variable costs, since a company that prices below variable costs gets no contribution toward its fixed costs or profits), the ceiling on prices is normally set by the economic value perceived by customers specific to a market segment or niche. Let me illustrate. Economic value by customer (EVC) is defined as the maximum price a customer will pay for a product, given its potential economic savings stream, *before* it becomes economical to switch to another product or to a substitute. In a consumer market, for example, the price of house insulation is set so that the savings in energy costs over the years provide a payback on the insulation investment. The EVC, of course, can escalate as energy costs escalate. In this example, a different EVC is present for different methods of insulating (new windows, weather stripping, caulking, or fiberglass batting insulation), and such EVCs vary by customer segment (for instance, those with older, drafty homes have needs different from those with newer homes).

*Eileen Shapiro is president of the Hillcrest Group, Inc., a management consulting firm in Cambridge, Massachusetts.

Figure 4-4. The strategic triangle.

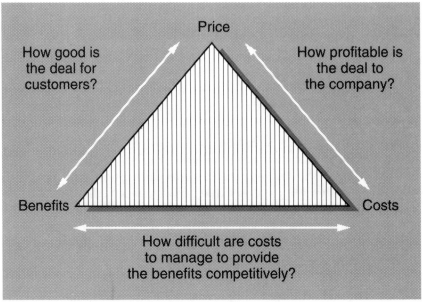

Source: Adapted from Eileen Shapiro, *How Corporate Truths Become Competitive Traps* (New York: John Wiley & Sons, 1991), Chapters 4–6.

This same EVC principle exists in industrial markets and acts as a ceiling on pricing. For example, Kevlar, a product of DuPont, is a fiber that on a per-unit-weight basis is five times as strong as steel. So a thin strand of Kevlar can support very heavy weights. When DuPont was looking for Kevlar applications, one area it looked at was using Kevlar in electrical transmission cables to replace steel (which, when wrapped in aluminum, conducts electricity). This could greatly lighten cables. Kevlar, however, is far more expensive per pound than steel cable. So DuPont could not convince electrical engineers that they could get economic value from steel substitution despite Kevlar's features. For general electrical transmission line usage, Kevlar would have to be priced so low that DuPont would have no return on its sale. However, in electrical transmission in mountainous areas, customers did have a high EVC for Kevlar in cabling because it could save the utility money by allowing it to use lighter and fewer (that is, spaced at greater distances) transmission towers. This would also cut construction costs in mountainous areas because these towers had to be flown in and put in place using expensive helicopters. EVC, as a technique, allows a company to maximize its pricing yield by finding those segments of a market in which EVC is high enough to sustain pricing at a profit.

EVC can be a broad and useful concept in a great many markets. For example, Kaufman and Broad Home Corporation, one of California's top home builders, raised its share of the market during the recent recession from 2.7 percent to 4 percent by lowering its prices on starter homes. Its average price was cut from $196,000 to $160,000 to provide an economic value attractive enough to home or apartment renters to induce them to purchase a new home. By pricing right per segment, Kaufman and Broad was able to grow while the sales of other builders around them declined. And its profits also increased markedly through lowering the ceiling on starter-home prices to a level at which potential buyers felt they could shift from renting to owning their own home.[3]

The concept of EVC is particularly apt in pricing new products. For example, when cellular phones were first marketed, it was a very expensive luxury to both purchase the phone and pay for line-use charges. In fact, the economic value to a customer could only be justified in specific use applications where the convenience of car phoning had a direct, quantifiable benefit. The two segments in which this was the case were contractors, to whom "time is money," and real estate salespeople, whose ability to handle multiple clients while on the go could double their productivity in showing houses and closing house sales for commissions.

Over time, as phone prices and line charges dropped, other segments of the market have found that cellular phones have a justifiable economic value. These include businessmen and sales reps, whose alternatives used to be using public telephones or phones at their customers' offices. To illustrate how lower prices trigger an increase in users, Figure 4-5 graphs the number of U.S. subscribers and the revenues from cellular phone sales over a five-year period. As can be calculated, subscriber costs were higher in 1987 at $1,000 per year per subscriber than they were in 1991 at $759 per year per subscriber.

It is frequently critical with new products to find the EVC that

Figure 4-5. Cellular phone subscribers and revenues, 1987–1991.

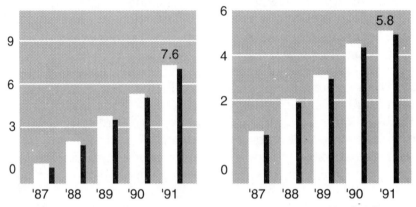

Source: Data reported by Peter Cox, "Not Just a Yuppie Toy," in *Business Week* (February 24, 1992), p. 36.

brings as many new customers on board as quickly as possible. Typically, however, the lack of developed demand for new products does not allow for the scale economies of mass production. As a result, companies often start at high prices and work these down lower, bringing on board more customers whose EVC is triggered by the lower price.

This is precisely AT&T's situation as it tries to market its new Videophone 2000, a telephone that permits the user to both hear and see the other party. Its $1,499 price is far too high to interest the mass market; in fact, surveys show that people want a price closer to $225 per phone before they will purchase it.[4] Until the EVC trigger levels are approached with lower prices, this new product won't generate big volumes.

When a small change in price elicits a big change in demand, a product is said to have high elasticity of demand, while those in which price changes elicit little change in volume sales are usually labeled "price-inelastic." Knowing the elasticity of demand greatly assists a company in optimally managing its incentivizing system and getting the best yield from price. Once VCRs and microwaves were priced low enough, huge markets opened up to them, and mass adoption began. In fact, microwaves are sufficiently low in price today that many homes (over 12 percent in the United States) have two per household. Knowing price elasticity and EVC requires that companies do market research to determine trigger price points per market segment. Failure to do this research on a segment basis can lead to across-the-board average pricing, in which some segments pay less than they would be willing to, whereas others feel the price is too high given their sensitivities. For example, a chain of day-care centers operating in both middle-class suburbs and economically disadvantaged inner-city neighborhoods would do well to have tiered pricing based on the different price sensitivities of their two different markets. The use of average pricing would leave money on the table in the upscale market but lead to overcharging the financially hard-pressed market. When Gillette first priced its greatly successful Sensor razor, the company did a lot of price sensitivity research. The results indicated that Gillette should price the new razor cheaper than many other nondisposables ($3.75 each) so that disposable-razor users might consider switching, yet expensive enough to preserve a prestigious image for the new design.

Effective Product Line/Brand Equity Management

The last of the four factors (from Figure 4-2) that can have a dramatic impact on pricing yield is product line/brand equity management. In making pricing decisions, companies want to maximize the long-run profitability and share of market *for their whole line of products*, not merely for specific items in the line. Kodak prices its cameras low in order to sell as many as possible so as to get the follow-along higher-margin film sales. Gillette's Sensor razor blades at seventy-five cents each generate a 90 percent gross margin, so they are the major profit generator for the entire shaving system.

Supermarkets make little profit on bread sales but do well on English muffins and more upscale bakery items. AT&T includes basic black telephones in its line even though they are unprofitable. In many cases, the volumes sold of basic items (like the black telephone) in a line hold down costs of the specialty items because the shared components contained in all the line can be made in higher volume, thus lowering unit costs and boosting total line profitability. Effective product-mix selling usually involves marketing parts of the line at different price points connoting "good," "better," and "best" value. For instance, Hart, Schaffner and Marx sells suits in different price brackets with different brand names; its Hickey-Freeman suits are top of the line, while Pierre Cardin suits sell at the middle of the price range and Johnny Carson suits in the lower price range.

Maximizing pricing yield requires a company to test the upper reaches of price sensitivity by customer segment and "value" added.

Clearly, as the Hart, Schaffner and Marx example illustrates, a strong brand name telegraphs value to its specific intended segment. If a product has a well-defined brand image and position in the market, it can command loyalty in buying and sustain its chosen price position, whether this is the luxury, middle, or lower-end price position. Rolex and Longines do this in high-priced watches, Bulova and Seiko in moderately priced watches, and Timex and Swatch U.S.A. at the low-priced end. Johnson & Johnson's strong branded pain reliever Tylenol continues to dominate its market despite efforts by Excedrin and Datril to take market share. And Tylenol's dominance helps keep it from being priced too high. So powerful is the Tylenol brand's equity that it even regained its place in the market after the famous Tylenol poisoning/tampering cases occurred in the 1980s. High brand equity translates into the best possible prices because retailers provide strong brands with the best shelf space. In fact, a Marketing Science Institute-sponsored research project verified that brand extensions gain shelf space and customer trial at far less cost than is needed for a completely new product entry. Also, brand buyers are loyal in their repurchasing behavior (witness repeat buyers of Honda cars, Oreo cookies, Nabisco's Ritz crackers, or Levi's jeans). In addition, brand equity often allows for profitable spin-offs such as Mars frozen ice cream bars, Jello Pudding Pops, Weight Watchers frozen entrées, and Miller's Genuine Draft Beer.

Astute brand equity management can keep a brand dominating its market for many years. For instance, 3M's Scotch brand tape dominates in tape sales across much of the world, and is a product more than fifty years old. Nabisco's Shredded Wheat is over a hundred years old and still selling well. Brand dominance translates into pricing premiums versus competitors. This price premium can occur in the original sale *and*, in the case of some durables, in resales as well. Honda *used* cars command premiums over other comparably equipped used cars from other car manufacturers.

The Sony brand name in television sets, compact disc players, and other electronic products commands anywhere from a 10 to 20 percent price premium over other makers of televisions and stereo equipment such as Panasonic, Sharp, TDK, RCA, and Toshiba.

If effective pricing is as closely tied to effective brand equity as a Siamese twin, the issue clearly is how to keep brand equity high. Effective brands have distinct images, personalities, and associations. They develop these by the clever use of design (Braun appliances), symbols (McDonald's golden arches), colors (Campbell's red and white soup cans), logos (Lacoste's alligator), packaging (L'Eggs pantyhose), theme lines (HALLMARK—WHEN YOU CARE ENOUGH TO SEND THE VERY BEST), and a well-chosen name (Head and Shoulders shampoo).

But all the imagery, slogans, and design in the world are useless without powerful advertising to convey them and consistent, "contemporized" product performance that lives up to the benefits promised. Tide has been reformulated many times over to deliver on its promise of whiter clothes. It has had to be altered for different fabrics, washing machines, cold-water washing, and so on. Sony's Walkman has been "contemporized" in more than a hundred variations including those that are waterproof and solar-powered.

When Procter & Gamble saw its brand equity eroding through overpromotion and too much trade "dealing" with retail chain supermarkets, it decided to redirect some of its promotion spending back into branded advertising and to lower its everyday prices. It reduced its list prices by anywhere from 10 to 25 percent rather than offer retailers a continuing succession of very rich promotions that teach consumers to wait for sales, dilute the brand's quality image, and reduce Procter & Gamble's available funds to do branded advertising to reinforce brand superiority.[5] Brand equity sustenance without reinforcement advertising or pull-through sales force efforts, for instance on prescription drug detailing of

physicians, won't work. IBM's failure to position and heavily advertise its OS/2 operating software as aggressively as did its rival, Microsoft, for its Windows operating software relegated OS/2 to a 10
percent market share versus Microsoft's 90 percent.

And companies must be cautious about assuming they can
brand-extend and get a price premium in any market. Brand equity doesn't always yield the same dividend in every segment. Gillette's Lady Atra, a branded line extension of its men's Atra razor
system, did not succeed with women in getting either a strong
brand position or a price premium versus Schick's Personal Touch
lady's razor system.[6] Women don't shave every day as men do, and
they continue to prefer using disposable razors until these no
longer feel sharp, at which point they throw them out. Brand equity can also change over time as the result of consumer attitude
shifts. In 1991, Levi's 501 Jeans sales grew by more than 20 percent because during the tough economic recession consumer loyalty to this branded jean increased, while loyalty to jean brands
priced $60 per pair and higher dropped. The net result was that
Levi Strauss sales topped $4.9 billion in 1991, up 16.7 percent
from 1990, in large part owing to brisk sales of its more basic blue
jeans lines.

Astute Discount Schedule Design

When marketers design price discount schedules to induce optimum ordering and motivation of their wholesalers, distributors,
dealers, or retailers, they must decide on five key issues:

1. What is the minimum order quantity?
2. How many volume purchase-level price discount breaks
   will they build into their plan?
3. What will the percentage off list price be at each volume
   discount break? And will these price breaks be equal in
   proportion as volumes increase?
4. Will additional rebates be paid to the dealer or distributor
   on the basis of annualized volumes?
5. What will the maximum discount be in terms of dealer order size? In other words, at what volume per order or per
   annualized purchases will discount levels no longer increase in percentage?

For instance, per order maximums can be set for a "truck-load," while maximum discounts may occur at a million dollars in annual purchases. Too high a minimum order quantity will eliminate some smaller dealers from ever buying at less than list price. Too many different volume breaks result in chaotic ordering and lots of order errors, since dealers are constantly moving up and down the schedule in keeping with normal sales fluctuations. Too few breaks, in which higher order discounts can be earned only with very large order sizes, may demotivate dealers since very few would qualify for the next level of discount through their normal growth in sales. Given that such extra discounts are beyond their reach, dealers could seek to be supplied by competitors with more reasonably attainable price/volume inducement levels.

It usually makes sense if the volume order levels set to motivate dealer ordering are in sync with the preferred production plans or ideal shipping units of the company. Sony's experience illustrates this point. When Sony first began making transistor radios, its president, Akio Morita, approached a large U.S. chain retailer with the product. The chain loved the radios and asked Sony for price quotes on 5,000, 10,000, 25,000, 50,000, and 100,000 radios. The chain fully expected the price per radio to be lower as its order volume escalated. However, Morita was not sure he could stretch Sony's capacity to produce 100,000 radios at a time without starving other markets of the product. While this was a tempting short-term way of gaining sales, Morita thought it would harm Sony's future with other distribution channels in other markets. So what did he do? He quoted his prices as follows: 100,000 radios per order cost the *highest* price per unit, an order of 50,000 came a little lower, while the best unit price was at 10,000 units per order. This was better than the price for 5,000 units per order. The buyer thought Morita was crazy, but he placed an order for 10,000 radios, which was exactly what Morita wanted. Morita opened up many other retailers globally with the same price discount strategy and assured himself of Sony meeting its production targets *and* opening the broadest possible distribution channels for Sony's transistor radios.[7]

The case of a Canadian publisher illustrates how a poor discount design can lead to a major retail fiasco. The publisher came out with a popular four-volume set of encyclopedias at a suggested retail price of $175 per set. However, huge discounts for very large volume orders were built into its price schedule. Canada's two large chain bookstores bought the set at $75 and decided to sell it at $99 per set. The smaller, independent bookstores, the publisher's most loyal clientele, could only buy the encyclopedias at $125 per set, given their volume order sizes. They had figured on selling the set at or close to the publisher's suggested retail price of $175. But when people realized the set could be obtained for less than $100 from the chain stores, they flocked to them, and the independents could not lower their price sufficiently to compete, since their *buying* price was $125 per set. They returned all the sets to the publisher along with hundreds of nasty complaint letters about the publisher's price strategies. They subsequently boycotted several of this same publisher's later books. This situation could have been avoided had the publisher maintained a less steep discount policy for giant orders.

Variable Rebates for Growth or Product Mix Sales

One effective tactic in pricing to induce dealer behavior of the kind a company desires is to provide volume discount rebates paid on a sliding scale, depending on the growth in purchases over the previous year's purchases. By setting rebate levels cleverly, a company can self-liquidate these. That is, the extra growth in purchases more than pays for the extra percentages granted in discounts. If a company sells a number of product lines and wants to induce the dealer to order a wide mix of the products offered, rebate percentage levels can be stepped up on the basis of whether only one product in the desired mix is bought, two are bought, three are bought, and so forth. In effect, the buyer who stocks the full line gets a considerable multiplier effect on its rebates as a result of such a commitment. Each of these tactics is designed to sell a desired mix of products and to reward the dealer for the extra effort in really growing sales in total and across the whole product line.

Creativity in Incentivizing Systems

Inducing customers (whether distributor customers or end-user customers) to purchase with incentives is a very old game. Coupons and rebates have been used to good effect for many years, as have money-back guarantees, lifetime warranties on products, trade-in programs, and green stamp plans. Recently, frequent buyer or user discount plans have taken center stage with airlines, hotels, and retailers. These so-called frequent buyer plans reward purchasers with credits redeemable on future purchases, travel, or merchandise in catalogs. Some hotel programs offer extra value-added services to frequent users. For example, Ambassador East in Chicago offers VIPet service—you and your pampered pet are allowed to stay if you are a preferred, frequent user of the hotel. Frequent users of Four Seasons hotels are given coloring books and crayons for the kids, while Hyatt offers frequent visitors price reductions if their grandparents stay as well. One incentivizing tactic hotels have borrowed from airlines is to offer reduced rates on rooms booked fourteen to twenty-one days in advance, but on a nonrefundable basis. Marriott sold 250,000 rooms this way in 1991, 130,000 more than the chain would have sold without the inducement.[8]

Automobile manufacturers, which have offered factory rebate schemes for years, are also becoming more creative. General Motors in February 1992 offered to match rebates its suppliers were providing to their employees as incentives to buy General Motors cars. For instance, if XYZ Bumper Company offered $500 to an employee to buy a General Motors car, General Motors would match this rebate for ninety days.[9] Volkswagen knew that the recession was scaring people away from making big-ticket purchases such as cars. So it offered a new Payment Protection Plus program, which ensured that anyone buying or leasing a Volkswagen before March 31, 1992, could stop worrying about making payments if they were laid off. Volkswagen would pick up the tab of up to $500 per month for a total of twelve months under the plan. This unique plan showed considerable marketing ingenuity and courage in the face of cover stories in national magazines such as *U.S. News & World Report* headlined "Is Your Job Safe?"

Another novel pricing plan to induce better car sales is being tried by Ford on its Escort car series. In March 1992, Ford was selling its Escort line at one price for all four models of sedan, three-door and five-door hatchbacks, and its station wagon. Normally, each model has a different price, with the wagon the most expensive. Traditional car industry practice has been to set high sticker prices and then to discount for customers who bargain by model. The one-price strategy resulted in less haggling *and* a better deal on, for instance, the station wagon, which was worth $1,000 more than the sedan, yet carried the same price tag. Escort wagon sales did very well (40 percent of the mix of dealer sales versus the usual 17 percent), and sales of the total Escort line also did well. Apparently customers preferred less dickering over price once they were sure that Ford's basic price represented a fair deal.[10] Saturn has adopted this same tactic of setting sticker prices low and asking dealers not to dicker. That way, the focus is on selling the car, not "the deal." Sales of Saturn cars *per dealer* are four times that for mainstream GM car dealers.

Fast food restaurants use novel incentivizing systems when they offer combination meals at a set price that is lower than the individual items add up to. McDonald's offers Extra Value Meals and Burger King its BK Meal Deals, both of which offer a sandwich, french fries, and a soft drink at one low combination price. This tactic works exceptionally well on products bought as a system, whether this is food, a stereo/speaker system, or a personal computer with software, a modem, and a printer.

A great many industrial companies that sell numerous products to large retailers or wholesalers such as Wal-Mart offer combinability privileges to help chains obtain price discount levels. That is, the vendor allows the chain to order mixed carloads or pallets comprised of quite varied products, all of which count toward volume discounts, rather than requiring order minimums of each product before maximum discounts are obtained. This tactic incentivizes the retailer to add items to orders because each item's volume augments the account's total purchase levels and results in top discounts or rebates at year end or per quarter.

Avoiding Needless Complexity and Building in Incentivizing System Flexibility

When pricing systems are complex, pricing errors occur on orders and customer confusion often results. In fact, the sales force too often becomes confused if pricing is too complicated.

Consider the case of automobile options. Not too many years ago, the option combinations it was possible to order for an automobile resulted in pricing combinations in the millions. In fact, before Chrysler simplified matters, its Omni car had eight million pricing combinations possible. Chrysler decided to make several options standard, and then, as did many other automobile manufacturers, it bundled packages of options together so that only four or five packages were available. The pricing combinations were reduced to fewer than forty from more than 8 million. This type of pricing tactic change is much more consistent with getting pricing right the first time and with avoiding errors in communicating prices to customers and in writing up the order. Ford's one-price system for its Escort series is a further simplification of a system that even dealers found confusing. Simplification of one system in marketing often has very beneficial effects on others. Clearly, when pricing is simplified for cars, advertising related to car prices is also simplified, as is selling the cars in the showroom. So a change in the pricing system results in more efficient showroom selling and car advertising in newspapers, on radio, via direct mailers, and on price stickers in the dealer's lot. Ford's one-price system also simplified its national advertising campaigns since it can advertise Escorts across all dealer regions with the knowledge that prices on dealer lots will be the same everywhere.

While simplicity is a valuable attribute of incentivizing systems, some flexibility is desirable to accommodate customer differences. For instance, Nintendo of America, the video game market leader, used to incentivize its retail channels by offering two separate promotional allowances, one that could be spent for co-op advertising on Nintendo's products and a separate one for merchandising displays, fixtures, or catalogs. As Nintendo's retail mix of channels shifted from mostly toy stores to mass merchants, software outlets, and other consumer product stores, this system proved too rigid, since some channels wanted mostly merchandising support moneys while others wanted mostly co-op ad moneys. As a result, Nintendo changed its incentivizing plan to allow retailers to earn a pool of funds (based on their purchase levels), which each retailer can use for either purpose in whatever mix it desires for its store.

The Importance of Timing and Measurement to Pricing Yield

In a great many marketing situations, capturing revenue from a price increase is a function of timing. In seasonal markets or markets in which products are sold via catalog, it is vital, if prices are to increase, that these prices be adjusted well in advance of the key sales season or the catalog's printing. An increase in price after this critical "timing window" is useless as a revenue generator. This often requires that a company forecast its costs well into the future so that it will know well in advance of such timing windows if it will require a hike in price or a drop in price (if it anticipates costs falling). In addition, with many wholesalers and dealers on computerized inventory systems, dealers often ask for thirty to sixty days' advance notice of price changes in order to reload the product pricing files into their own computer records.

The best possible pricing yield is also a function of effective price tracking systems. The company that keeps an ongoing record of tender pricing wins and losses, and graphs this data, can usually improve its tendering batting average because competitor pricing patterns can be visualized. Accounting systems that mon-

---

Figure 4-6. Tactics to maximize pricing yield.

✓ Know your competitiveness index.

✓ Go for maximum price yield per market segment.

✓ Have a cost strategy in mind if you must lower pricing.

✓ Be able to justify your price's economic value to the customer (EVC).

✓ Keep brand equity high for maximum price premiums versus rivals.

✓ Design price discounts astutely so that they motivate resellers.

✓ Use variable rebates that reward specific goals in growth or sales mix.

✓ Try creativity in incentives.

✓ Watch price timing.

✓ Avoid too much pricing complexity.

✓ Don't make incentives too rigid.

✓ Track pricing so that you can make mid-course corrections fast.

---

itor the percentage of volumes sold by percentage "off list" brackets can trend their pricing and adjust either discounting policies or list prices on the fly. Midcourse corrections in pricing are more important than in the past because shortened product life cycles have raised the risks inherent in mispricing a product for even a short time. Good tracking of pricing is akin to operating with good radar on board an aircraft. By staying informed of where the pricing storm clouds are at all times, the company knows when to dive lower with prices and when to bring prices to a higher altitude.

Figure 4-6 lists tactics that are effective in maximizing pricing yield and moving toward zero-defect pricing.

Notes

1. Bill Saporito, "Why the Price Wars Never End," *Fortune* (March 23, 1992), pp. 74, 78.
2. Allan J. Magrath, "Ten Timeless Truths About Pricing," *The Journal of Consumer Marketing*, Vol. 8, No. 1 (Winter 1991), pp. 5–13.
3. Kathleen Kerwin, "The Sturdy House That Kaufman and Broad Built," *Business Week* (February 17, 1992), p. 122.
4. "AT&T Introduces the First Color Video Phone for Home Use," *Washington Post* (January 7, 1992), pp. C1–C2.
5. Zachary Schiller, "Not Everyone Loves a Supermarket Special," *Business Week* (February 17, 1992), pp. 64–66.
6. "Gillette Company Tries to Sell Sensor to Women," *Market Week* (Febuary 24, 1992), p. 8.
7. Jack Nadel, "Distribution, the Key to Success Overseas," *Management Review* (September 1987), p. 42.
8. "Selling Hotel Rooms Like Airline Tickets," *Travel Agent Magazine* (September 23, 1991), p. 76.
9. Harris Collingwood, "What's Good for General Motors is Good for Us All?" *Business Week* (February 24, 1992), p. 42.
10. "Ford Motor Takes Its One-Price Nationwide," *The Wall Street Journal* (March 12, 1992), pp. B1, B5.

5

The Product Innovation System

These are difficult days for auto manufacturers; they're thinking up ways to make their products safer and new names to make them sound more dangerous.

Thomas La Mance

In 1990, Kodak opened a new, graphics technology product center in London and announced plans for another center, this one for clinical products, in Strasbourg, France. Each center will include marketing, customer support, and customer training facilities, and each supports Kodak's thrust to move closer geographically to its customers as a way of stimulating embryonic ideas and of expanding and exploiting existing new products. Royal Dutch Shell developed and introduced a new environmentally enhanced gasoline (SU 2000E) in under three months, versus its normal twelve-month development cycle time in 1990. Shell also introduced two innovative resins in this time frame (from its chemical division) into the electronics market in only half the time it normally took Shell to do this.

Amp, a world leader in connectors for industry, has boosted the yield from its innovation system via customer partnering with huge clients such as Boeing. Amp created a new connector (and a lightweight tooling system to apply the connectors) for Boeing's new airplane that can be used in everything from the complex wiring of navigational instruments to wiring devices and connectors for in-flight movies. Amp's innovativeness with customer partnering has helped its sales to grow beyond $3 billion worldwide.

In all three of these cases, the companies were looking to process improvements to boost either the yield or the responsiveness of their new product systems. Kodak is doing it by getting nearer its customers, Amp by partnering with selected key accounts, and Shell by emphasizing response-time improvements in new product generation. These companies have seized on key process variables they believe need improvement and then have applied the resources necessary to get better performance. C. K. Prahalad, a world-renowned expert in management and professor of strategic management at the University of Michigan, put it succinctly when he said, "More money on research and development is money down a rat hole if you don't change the process."[1]

There is no doubt that new products (or services) are the lifeblood of many companies. They allow for expanded total markets, rapid market penetration, and above-average market pricing since customers value, in dollars and cents, the new product's uniqueness and edge over competitive offerings. So it is no wonder that as corporations strive for total quality they are turning their attention to continuous improvement in yield rates on new products from research labs, or are looking to cut the time to commercialization with so-called pacing programs. These identify the best new products on the development list and pour resources into getting them off the ground in the shortest possible cycle time.

Innovation System Components

The four major components of innovation systems are illustrated in Figure 5-1.

First, there is the generation or adoption of new product ideas, which may come from lab experiments, customer inputs, or licensing. In some cases, outright acquisition or joint ventures may produce ideas and/or finished new products. Second, the innovation system must manage the ideas and development efforts in some sort of structure, whether this be in the form of lab teams, cross-functional product development groups (including product managers from marketing), or under the auspices of the research and development department's technical management. Third, the new products, once designed and tested, must be commercialized. This

Figure 5-1. The product innovation system.

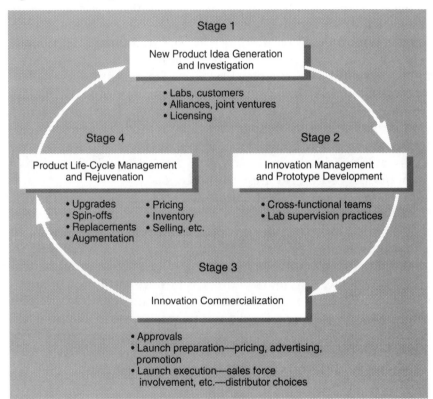

involves everything from sales force training to naming, packaging, and labeling approvals, in addition to other approvals related to introductory advertising, test marketing, sales literature, customer sampling, publicity releases, and third-party product testing endorsements (such as an Underwriter Laboratories certification). Finally, the innovation system involves managing the product over its life cycle, deciding on pricing, inventory, and sales forecast levels and on modifications to the line such as new variants on sizing, construction, or features. These last activities involve mainstream marketing management personnel.

To boost its speed in bringing product innovation to market while holding down costs, a company must decide whether its efficiencies in time and money ought to be sought in the idea generation stage, the management stage, the commercialization stage, or the exploitation stage. In order for Xerox to catch up to rival Canon in new copying products, it concentrated on faster management of product design (stage 2 in Figure 5-1), using concurrent engineering. It cut the number of part numbers per product prototype and began to revamp product planning so that it emulated the Japanese at Canon, who make variants on existing products using tested, mature technologies, and by so doing keep incrementally improving products and moving them to market quicker.[2] Successive generations of the product are given innovations in feature or are reduced in cost rather than starting out as "clean-sheet from-scratch" designed products. Other companies, such as Chrysler, use alliance partners such as Mitsubishi to create and bring new products to market on their behalf, concentrating on stage 1 of the process. 3M focuses on merging many different technologies (stage 2) to create new products that are hybrids of such formerly distinct technologies. For instance, its electronics technology and adhesives technology produced stick-on electrode monitors for stress testing in hospitals and clinics. Its adhesives and abrasives technology combined to produce sticky-backed abrasive discs, which are easily removed from sanders used in automotive body shop sanding. Its film and microabrasives technologies were combined to produce ultra-fine sanding discs used by dentists.

Gatorade has concentrated its product innovation efforts on stage 4 by adding flavors, different packaging (bottles versus powdered), and new sizes to fit different selling channels such as convenience stores, health clubs, vending machines, and supermarkets. Procter & Gamble similarly works at stage 4, freshening its product yields by using new technology to create superconcentrated liquid detergents and superabsorbent disposable diapers— in other words, better variations of mature products. Every company must look hard at all four stages of the product innovation process and decide which stage is most in need of improvement and what system factors count most (cycle time, cost, yield, and so on). The Japanese are increasingly organizing their systems so that they can produce three new products for every one of their current products. One is often a significant improvement on the current product, say, at a lower cost or with more features, such as a faster copier. The second is often an offshoot of the current product, such as a compact tabletop personal copier. Yet a third may be a genuine new leapfrog offering, such as a full-color copier. The Japanese by pursuing multiple product replacements for their current offerings are trying to make themselves obsolete before their competitors do it for them.

As shown in Figure 5-2, companies in the last few years have increasingly selected two somewhat neglected aspects of the innovation process, namely, process flexibility and environmental impact, to improve.

Flexibility

There has been heightened attention paid in recent years to the ability of corporations to customize new marketing offerings by account or consumer need. In Japan, for instance, Toyota buyers can select what they want from a variety of combinations of features and colors on a Monday morning and pick up their new car no later than Friday afternoon.[3]

Motorola can handle pagers, customized to order, in several million feature combinations and ship finished products within two hours of when the product was demanded. Telecommunication companies that add data bases can often add a variety of services to exploit the data base's use, from electronic mail to mail order catalogs to airline booking services and so forth.

At one time, innovation in new products required limited complexity in order to focus the product line's production and gain scale cost efficiencies. High variety went hand in hand with high cost. This is no longer the case with automated, numerically controlled factory processes. As a result, product innovation systems have a broader scope for creative offerings. For instance, Matsushita Electric's subsidiary, the National Bicycle Industrial Company, sells bikes under Matsushita's Panasonic brand name. Customers who purchase a Panasonic bike can specify their favorite color, size, model (racing, road, or mountain bike), and design. The customer's spec is faxed to Panasonic's bike factory and a computer generates a blueprint of the bike. Robots then measure, cut, weld, and paint the frame to match the order. Skilled workers apply any

Figure 5-2. Process variables of the innovation system.

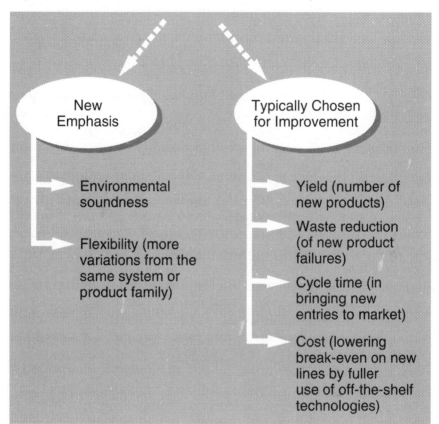

New Emphasis

- Environmental soundness
- Flexibility (more variations from the same system or product family)

Typically Chosen for Improvement

- Yield (number of new products)
- Waste reduction (of new product failures)
- Cycle time (in bringing new entries to market)
- Cost (lowering break-even on new lines by fuller use of off-the-shelf technologies)

finishing touches, such as decals, or special parts and even silk-screen each customer's name on the bicycle frame. More than ten million different customized bikes can be made this way at a price not significantly higher than that of standard ten-speed bicycles.

As companies examine their innovation systems, they ought to carefully consider the flexibility dimension of product design customization. Flexibility allows the company to operate in markets of high turbulence, where customer needs are highly varied, technological change rates are high, and the existence of substitutes to satisfy the market abounds.

Lutron Electronics Company is the dominant market share leader in lighting controls for homes and offices, yet 95 percent of its products are shipped in units of fewer than 100. Furthermore, it has never shipped the same electronic lighting system twice.

Environmental Impact

While a process mind-set in marketing as applied to new products has resulted in higher variety, shorter development times, and greater yields, the environmental impact of innovation systems is only beginning to be examined. Producing lots of varied new products in record time from an innovation system is not helpful if their generation results in product use, product design, product disposal, product transportation and handling, or product production that harms the environment. Design must take account of energy use, safety, toxicity, and renewable resource consumption. Product disposal ought to favor reusability, returnability, degradability, or recyclability. Product distribution ought to allow for safe product transport, storage, and handling. The product's production process ought to minimize harmful emissions or wasteful energy use and result in minimal throw-away packaging. Record makers are working very hard to find compact disc packaging that is less harmful to the environment than their "jewel box," hard plastic exterior packaging.

Lever Brothers, in the United States, is marketing more concentrated detergents that use organic compounds, are boxed in recycled paperboard, and can be recycled again. In fact, the concentrated nature of the new product in terms of its greater cleaning power and smaller volume saves total packaging mass as compared with the less concentrated bulk detergent cleaners from Lever.

General Electric markets an entire line of Energy Choice light bulbs that save energy by using a 52-watt bulb in place of a 60-watt bulb while providing equivalent brightness. Manufacturers of small nickel-cadmium batteries have created a huge problem for themselves due to the success of these long-life batteries. The toxic effects of dumping the batteries in landfill sites are coming back to haunt the manufacturers because they insufficiently considered the environmental impact of their product once it entered the "waste stream."

Boosting New Product Yields by Way of Licensing

Growing a company with new products, all of which emanate from its own ingenuity, can be risky. The imperative to grow may outstrip innate, organic creativity, and stagnant sales can set in. It may then make sense to license new products from others. In the pharmaceutical industry, drugs are frequently licensed for sale by one company from the original drug formula discovery company. In Canada, some of the best-selling beers are licensed for production by Canadian brewers such as Labatt and Molson—from Elders in Australia and from Anheuser-Busch, Coors, or Miller Brewing in the United States. In some instances, it is not even necessary to license a product or concept; rather, the license of a brand name alone can boost sales and bring "uniqueness" to otherwise ordinary offerings.

For example, the Helen of Troy Corporation was a leading marketer of hair-care appliances (hair dryers, curling irons, and so forth) for professional salons in America. Sales had gone flat and the company wanted to grow by moving into consumer retail markets for these same products. Yet it had almost no consumer brand identity of the kind Gillette or Clairol could boast. So Helen of Troy licensed the Vidal Sassoon brand name for a royalty fee and applied it to its new consumer offerings. Sales moved from $10 million in 1980 to $117 million in 1990, and its Sassoon branded curling irons, hair dryers, and hot curlers are now first or second in their respective markets in the United States.

Major League Baseball Properties, Major League Baseball's licensing arm, licenses its logos and team designs for use on more than 3,000 items. Retail sales of these licensed items exceed $1.8 billion, earning the league $75 million per year, or $2.6 million per team. In a similar vein, Spiegel, the $2-billion-a-year catalog and specialty store operation, now markets a line of boys' and girls' clothing using the licensed brand name Crayola from Binney & Smith, the crayon people.

Analysis Factors for Sorting Out Options

Applying process variables for product development alternatives can be highly instructive. For instance, Figure 5-3 illustrates a

Figure 5-3. Research and development management options for new products.

Process Variable	Research and Development Alliances (with others)	Do All Your Own Research and Development Centrally	Do All Your Own Research and Development But Decentralize
Cost	Medium	High	High
Efficiency	Medium	High	Medium
Responsiveness (cycle time on new products)	High	Medium	High
Controllability	Low-Medium	High	Medium

Considering Two Options

Current Alternative

comparison a company might make using system analysis factors. The company is considering trying to improve its product innovation system yield either by entering into research and development alliances with others or by decentralizing its research and development to multiple sites.

Corning is an example of a company that uses research and development alliances aggressively to develop new products from glass (silica) technology. For instance, by way of alliances, Corning has developed silicone with Dow Chemical (Dow-Corning) and fiberglass insulation with Owens (Owens-Corning). Using the key criteria of cost, controllability, efficiency, and responsiveness, the company can sort out its options and the trade-offs it faces. If it decentralizes research and development by site, it faces some loss of efficiency (through the duplication of some facilities and processes) and controllability (since it must now manage multiple research and development labs at some distance from its headquarters and from each other). If it is concerned about such losses in efficiency or controllability, it must look to some positive offset—

possibly greater responsiveness, as offsite labs can be located closer to market centers and customers. As an example, 3M has product development centers for automotive products centered in Detroit and in Germany and Japan, the two other centers of car design.

If the company examines the option of alliances, it clearly sees its trade-offs (versus the status quo). By sharing costs with a partner (a plus), it loses some controllability yet gains responsiveness since it may, via the alliance, be able to put its skills together with a partner's complementary skills and move a product idea to market much faster than it would by doing everything itself. This grid could be expanded to bring in other system dynamic variables, such as capacity (to generate new products) or complexity (the need to manage disparate locations and people). It might discover that these also vary by research and development option.

This kind of process analysis has helped companies such as IBM and Apple to sort out the necessity to joint-venture on new products, considering the capacity constraints in go-it-alone research and development strategies and the improvement potential in responsiveness so critical in the fast-moving computer industry. In fact, Apple and IBM's joint venture allows Apple to concentrate more on software development while sourcing more of its hardware needs from IBM.[4]

Toro, the Minnesota manufacturer of lawn mowers and specialized lawn equipment for golf courses, fosters innovation by paying independent inventors a retainer for their ideas. One of Toro's retained inventors, Bob Comer, came up with a revolutionary design for a golf green aerator that uses water jets to aerate the grass as opposed to the standard technology that loosens soil via metal pipes (which leave a messy trail of small dirt piles after aeration).

Managing the System for Mature Brands

When a company's sales soften, it is often confronted with having to consider how sounder management of its existing, mature products might reinvigorate its growth curve. This pressure can make itself felt when new products are stalled in the lab or penetrating the market or distribution more slowly than originally anticipated.

For instance, only 31 of some 220 U.S. cereal brands have shares of one percent or more, the same number as in 1985, when there were only 145 brands. So new products in this industry have not captured the public's fancy at all.

Given this factor, companies often turn to rejuvenating stale brands. Tums did this successfully from 1985 to 1991. In 1985, Rolaids had a 34 percent share of the antacid tablet market versus Tums's 19 percent. Then Tums decided to play up the fact that its formulation of calcium carbonate was sodium-free, as opposed to Rolaids, which contained a lot of sodium. In the six years following the advertisement of this news, Tums's share not only caught up with but actually surpassed Rolaids.

Exploiting timely concerns, newly relevant to consumers, is just one of many ways of focusing on mature brand rejuvenation. Mars rejuvenated sales by applying its brand names and candy flavor formulas to ice cream products. Reebok launched an offshoot of its performance athletic shoes to appeal to more "life-style-oriented" buyers who want a less pricey, more casual shoe. Called Boks, the shoes come in subdued colors, with handsome stitching, and look more like shoes from L. L. Bean or Timberland than from Reebok.

Procter & Gamble is successfully rejuvenating sales of Pepto-Bismol by targeting it for a new use—as a treatment for traveler's diarrhea. The same company is also resurrecting sales of Oil of Olay by retargeting it to younger women as a moisturizing skin treatment rather than as a wrinkle protector for women over forty.

Berlitz International has boosted its mature sales of language phrase books and travel guides by going electronic. It licenses its name on a palm-size electronic gadget that translates typed-in words and phrases into five languages for travelers.

In every case, the overriding concern of these companies was for enhanced yield from their mature brands through repositioning and unique offshoots.

Another potent way to boost yield from mature brands is to give them fresh appeal in a new packaging design. Kaytee Products of Chilton, Wisconsin, has been selling wild bird seed for 120 years, and sales never exceeded $10 million per year across America. In 1986, the company brought in a Chicago-based package design firm in an attempt to move its drab packaging into a more upscale, artsy design phase. Kaytee was interested in trying this in order to get into pet food stores and supermarkets in addition to the hardware stores that already represented its main distribution channel.

The designers came up with a package depicting brightly colored birds against a beautiful forest to appeal to bird feeders to treat their birds as backyard guests. The redesign shot Kaytee's sales upward to $90 million per year within six years of the implementation of the new package design.

When Kao redesigned their Jergens brand lotion bottle from the old yellow-necked package into an obelisk-shaped white package, its image moved to a classier, sleek look. Jergens sales have grown 30 percent since the change in 1991.

So whether the package design objective is to appeal to new distribution channels or to upgrade a product's image, it can greatly expand the sales yield from mature product lines.

Product Innovation System Costs

The yield from product innovation systems is often erratic. New products or models do not sell as predictably as the sun coming up each morning. There is enormous pressure on such systems when the costs per new product escalate rapidly while at the same time the margins from previous product models are in decline. Risks mount higher while returns become less certain. This is the case for both Honda and Porsche. Porsche has allowed its product line to go stale, while others, including Toyota, Nissan, Mitsubishi, and Mazda, have offered up many new luxury sports cars. Porsche's last new model, the 928, was a 1978 engineered product, and its new four-door model will not be ready until the mid-1990s. As a result, its sales volume, dollar sales, and after-tax profits are in severe decline, as shown in Figure 5-4.

Honda's new product yield suffers from a quite different problem. It has failed to keep its market share either because its styling lacked flair or because it ignored "hot" new market niches in North America such as pickup trucks and vans. At the same time that its model yield has misfired, its profits have plummeted owing to the crippling rebate price wars going on in the United States.

Figure 5-4. Porsche's sales and profits, 1986–1991.

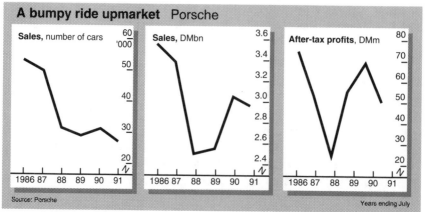

Source: "A Blowout in the Fast Lane," *The Economist* (September 21, 1991), p. 83. © 1991 The Economist Newspaper Group, Inc. Reprinted with permission.

For both Honda and Porsche, a still deadlier problem lurks. Although each company is rich in engineering talent, and each may be able to step up new product yield rates, the cost of engineering and equipping a factory to build a new model car has gone out of sight. The cost today is over $1 billion and still climbing as tougher safety and environmental standards boost unit costs per vehicle. In Porsche's case, the company may have to merge with Mercedes, Volkswagen, or BMW, while Honda will have to preserve its cash flow more carefully, possibly pulling out of expensive cash drains such as its Formula One racing sponsorship. Both companies illustrate the dilemma of playing catch-up on new products when the ante to produce a new product escalates and operating margins to fund such yield initiatives begin to dry up.

Innovation Tied to the Services Surrounding the Product

As companies look to the individual component parts of their innovation systems for better process management, sometimes it is necessary to stand back and decide if the problem is really centered in one of the four subcomponents at all. Often it is not. At

Xerox, for example, two of its biggest innovation system break-throughs were not product- or design-related. Xerox hooked the world on xerographic copying in large part by leasing its 914-model copiers rather than by selling them. Xerox sales moved from $2 million in 1960 to $59.5 million in 1961 and $428 million in 1966. The innovation of leasing the machines and charging on the basis of metered pricing was as revolutionary as the product itself. By setting a low base price that included a number of free copies, Xerox removed from many customers' minds the risk of trying the then-unproven xerographic technology. As utilization of the machines and customer acceptance grew, so too did Xerox's revenues and placements of the 914. Over the life of the machine, some 200,000 units were leased worldwide against initial Xerox forecasts of only 3,000 units.

A second innovation that has boosted Xerox sales is its three-year warranty "total satisfaction" plan. This plan replaces any machine for free—no questions asked—and is proving a powerful way of allowing Xerox to sell its more expensive, higher-tech products such as Docutech, a $220,000 machine that uses digital imaging. So far, the "total satisfaction" plan has resulted in only a handful of machines being returned by customers.[5] The issue of looking at more global fixes to innovation is conceptually illustrated in Figure 5-5.

In fact, a debottlenecking approach to a company's product innovation system may provide only marginal gains if it does not manage its reputation as well as its designs. North American automakers such as General Motors have lots of new car models, but selling them is very tough in the light of the poor market reputation that General Motors cars have had for so long. In an era of wide consumer choice, having lots of great new products is not enough; the company must also have a great image.

The Rewards of a Process Mind-Set

When a company manages its innovation systems with a view to yield, unit costs, cycle time, and flexibility, it can then apply these skills to innovations with the highest profit potential. The Japanese have demonstrated this fact over and over again. They have first

Figure 5-5. Two approaches to process improvement in innovation systems.

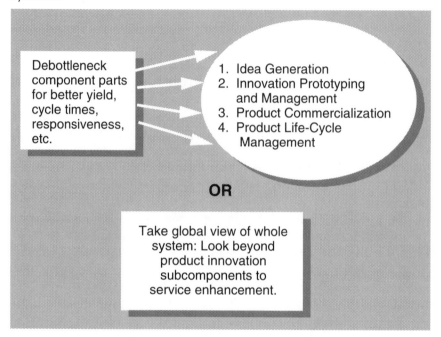

sought process improvements in low-end segments of the market, including watches, cameras, cars, small appliances, calculators, and copiers. Having mastered process breakthroughs in these low-end markets, they have then moved upmarket to luxury cars, high-tech cameras, color copiers, digital microwaves, and multifunction watches (with miniature TVs built in). By way of illustration, the Japanese use of concurrent engineering and fewer prototypes greatly cut development cycle times in new product commercialization (stage 3 in Figure 5-1). Having done so, not only could they look at more expensively featured products but they could even look to transferring this process mind-set to new product categories they had never before made. This was the case with Honda, which moved from motorcycles to small cars to lawn mowers. The Japanese pursuit of faster cycle times and greater yields from new products is fueled by their belief that they must make their own products obsolete before their rivals do it for them. As a result, they often try to produce multiple product models to replace each current model, investing as much time and money in this process as they previously put into producing one model. It was Sony that sounded the death knell for its own portable tape recorders with its Walkman.

An innovation system's ability to adapt and remain vital over time often depends on getting a continual flow of feedback from customers as to their needs. Johnson Controls of Milwaukee makes climate control systems for office buildings. As its customers began to voice their concerns about how costly Johnson Controls were to install and repair, Johnson set to work to overcome these objections. The result was a whole new line of equipment that uses interconnected modules that are easily replaced when the system goes down (as opposed to Johnson's older models, which required wiring to fix). Introduced in January 1990, the new line enjoyed sales in the first year of more than $500 million.

The Importance of Teamwork

Donald Frey, former vice president, product development, at Ford Motor Company, was in charge of overseeing a number of new products that revolutionized auto design. These included "lube for life" lubrication parts, disc brakes for cars, radial tires as standard equipment, and even the creation of the hugely successful Mustang model (in 1964). Frey learned early on the necessity of teamwork to produce innovation quickly and confidently.

Teams reduced the organizational barriers to innovation and eliminated the linear step-by-step approval processes in new product commercialization. A team of functional personnel creates what Frey calls a technology pool, in which engineering, marketing, manufacturing, sales, and purchasing can, at an early stage, share their knowledge and avoid unnecessary bureaucracy and hand-offs between departments that slow down planning.[6] Teams with the right mix of disciplines on them can meet tighter deadlines because design specs can be frozen in less time when the team members have authority and expertise across functions. In fact, Frey's team created the Mustang in eighteen months, a cycle time for new model design that was *still unmatched* in 1992 by either Detroit or Japanese car makers (in Japan, it takes three years for a new model creation/launch). Using a small cross-functional team, Rubbermaid created a brightly colored plastic storage container in which U.S. teenagers could store their compact discs. The product was produced in record time—before the company's competitors had a chance to come up with anything similar. It has been an enormous hit.

Innovation System Measurements

As more attention is paid to process improvement factors in innovation system analysis, there will follow along better measurements for use as benchmarks. For example, four key metrics are in use at Hewlett-Packard to measure progress in cycle time performance on new products. These are:

1. *Break-Even Time (BET)*—The time from the first investigation of a new product idea until product profits equal investment in development costs.

2. *Time-to-Market (TM)*—The total development time from the start of the development phase (stage 2 in Figure 5-1) until a product's release from manufacturing (stage 3 in Figure 5-1). Hewlett-Packard reduced TM on computer printers from 4.5 years to 22 months.

3. *Break-Even-After-Release (BEAR)*—The time from manufacturing release until the project investment costs are recovered in product profits. (Whereas TM measures research and development proficiency, BEAR tracks manufacturing/sales proficiency.)

4. *Return Factor (RF)*—The profit dollars divided by the investment dollars at an agreed-upon time after a product has moved into manufacture and sale. This can be used to compare returns by new product.

Bill Hewlett believed that you cannot manage what cannot be measured, so these measurements are evolving in use as Hewlett-Packard works hard to boost its innovation system yield (in profit and return) and cycle time (responsiveness in time).

Figure 5-6. Process improvement tactics for product innovation systems.

○ Design products in cooperation with customers.

○ Locate research and distribution centers near key markets/customers.

○ Work simultaneously on leap-frog new products and incremental change in products, and then decide which to push forward.

○ Innovate with flexible factory processes to boost new product variety and customization possibilities.

○ License new products from others.

○ Use new-product partnership alliances.

○ Hire independent inventors on a per-project basis.

○ Rejuvenate old products with new uses and new user targeting.

○ Add line extensions by means of sizing or package variations by trade channel.

○ Incorporate new technologies into existing products through new materials or formulas.

○ Augment products with new services that offer fresh appeals to price/value.

○ Use cross-functional, fast-moving teams for decision making and coordination of new product projects (or parts of projects).

○ Measure innovation progress routinely and in multiple ways.

When product innovation systems are modeled and measured, with process improvement analysis applied, new products often move faster to market as organizational rigidities are minimized. Marketing plays a key role in this in that customer needs, complaints, and concerns are often a fertile area in which to look for new product ideas, and marketing must play a major team role in idea development and commercialization. In stage 3 (mature brand rejuvenation), marketing is usually the lead player, as Xerox illustrated with its leasing and "total satisfaction guaranteed" marketing initiatives. With a process mind-set, marketers can look to customer complaints as a great source of innovation and can put in place market research and complaint systems tracking that recognize this fact. That is how Donald Frey was inspired to create grease-free fittings on cars: Customers had complained of not knowing when to grease their mechanical joints, and claimed that this was a real safety concern to them.[7]

A process mind-set in the key area of product innovation is helping to create more varied products at competitive costs. General Electric, for instance, standardized to fewer interchangeable parts, going from 28,000 to 1,275 on circuit breaker boxes. Costs per box fell by 30 percent, yet the process still produces 40,000 different sizes and shapes in boxes. In addition, this process helps companies such as IBM recognize when they should go outside their own organizations to license innovations from others as a faster way of competing. Putting outside suppliers on key product development teams is a variation on licensing. Navistar did this with suppliers such as Dana that make truck frames and axles. With suppliers' assistance, Navistar cut new product development time on a new truck for U-Haul by 50 percent—from 5 years to 2.5 years.

Figure 5-6 summarizes the many ways in which it is possible to increase the yield or responsiveness of product innovation systems.

Notes

1. Brian Dumaine, "Closing the Innovation Gap," *Fortune* (December 2, 1991), p. 62.
2. Mohan Kharbanda, "Back From the Brink," *CMA Magazine* (July-August 1991), p. 11.
3. S. Maital, "The Profits of Infinite Variety," *Across the Board* (October 1991), p. 7.
4. "Apple's Survival Plans," *The New York Times* (July 14, 1991), pp. F1, F6.
5. James R. Norman, "Xerox on the Move," *Forbes* (June 10, 1991), p. 71.
6. Donald Frey, "Learning the Ropes: My Life As a Product Champion," *Harvard Business Review* (September-October 1991), pp. 46–55.
7. *Ibid.*, p. 48.

6

The Channel System

The go-between wears a thousand sandals.

Japanese proverb

The astute management of distribution channels can often be the quality edge a company needs to dominate its industry. Hallmark dominates card sales by way of its extensive network of retailers and its company-owned specialty card shops. Steelcase's lead in office furniture sales is a direct result of its top-notch dealer system. Caterpillar Tractor and Coca-Cola globally dominate heavy construction equipment and soft drinks, respectively, in part because each has a world-class network—of dealerships in Caterpillar's case and of bottlers in Coke's case. And companies such as Nike, Levi Strauss, Duracell, and Black & Decker have leading shares in consumer markets because they make astute reseller choices and manage their complex, multiple retail channels with consistently solid supports. In effect, they all manage channel capacity decisions astutely and then work to keep channel yields at optimum levels.

Controlling channels often means controlling markets. For instance, in Japan, Toyota outsells Honda three and a half cars to one, and Nissan outsells Honda two to one. Yet in the United States, Honda has a market share equal to the larger overall Toyota, and Honda outsells Nissan two to one (with a 10 percent U.S. share versus Nissan's 5 percent). Why does Honda do so poorly in Japan? While it is not the complete answer, Honda's less successful Japanese share is greatly affected by its weaker dealer network. Because Honda is a younger company than either Toyota or Nissan, prime dealership sites in Japan were already controlled by its rivals when Honda began to manufacture its cars. Honda will not be able to best its competitors until it gets a more solid dealer network established in Japan. It is seeking to do just this by using its motorcycle dealer locations in Japan to sell cars as well as cycles. In the United States, where Honda and Toyota set up dealerships at roughly the same time, Toyota and Honda's shares are roughly equivalent, at 10 percent (for Honda) and 9 percent (for Toyota) respectively.

What Is a Channel System?

A channel system involves (1) a company's channel choices, (2) its decisions on channel supports, (3) the activities involved in channel monitoring and supervision, and (4) the company's actions to fine-tune and improve (1), (2), and (3) over time. Figure 6-1 illustrates a channel system conceptually. A company marketing its products or services may use a simple channel or a complex one to sell its offerings. For instance, airlines and hotels use travel agents, a simple, single-type of channel, to market their services. A company such as Coca-Cola uses a complex amalgam of channels, including all sorts of retailers, vending operators, and food service channels such as restaurants to market Coca-Cola. Of course, as channels increase in number and complexity, supports to them also have to be more varied and customized. Similarly, the monitoring and fine-tuning of channels is greatly affected by the channel's complexity. This is not to say that single, simple channels do not present management challenges to marketers. Witness the problems car manufacturers have getting their single, preferred, channel-independent dealerships to perform as car-driving customers would like them to (that is, with responsiveness, courtesy, ethics, and so forth) on a consistent basis. Nonetheless, complex channels do present real management problems to marketers because the channels' needs are so different from one another. So while a marketer such as Nike is keeping focused on end customers, runners, squash players, triathletes, and tennis players, it must also be aware of the different reseller marketing needs of specialty stores versus those of discounters, say, or even of its own factory outlets whose methods of merchandising, display, pricing, selling, and stocking are all quite varied.

Figure 6-1. Conceptualizing a marketing channel system.

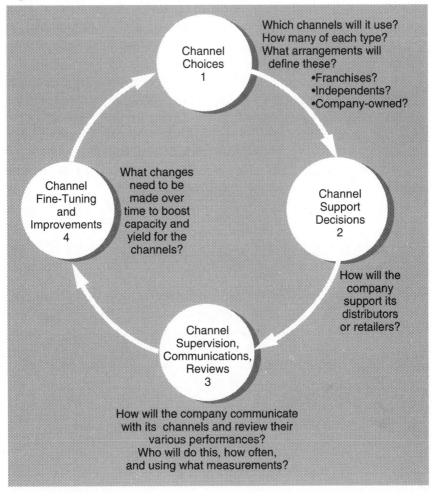

Continuous Improvement in Marketing Channel Management

Being good at managing channels over the long haul, in other words, continuously improving them for optimal brand share and customer satisfaction (both the reseller customers and the end customers), is a function of three elements, or key variables:

1. *Capacity.* Channel choices must match ongoing channel capacity to product demand and the needs of end customers. Too much capacity can lead to price wars, while too little can starve the market. The wrong kind of capacity can damage a brand's image or leave a market niche uncovered.

2. *Yield.* Supporting chosen channels involves boosting each so that the channel's yield is as high as possible. Having lots of channel capacity is useless if it doesn't yield sales and repeat business. In 1992, Rolls-Royce's U.S. sales were down 50 percent despite top-notch exclusive dealerships. Channel capacity was not its problem. Sales picked up only when Rolls-Royce helped its dealers with leasing-support financing so that auto-buying customers could avoid U.S. luxury taxes and afford the ongoing monthly payments.

3. *Efficiency.* Efficiency means fine-tuning channels so that the total channel costs are affordable—in other words, altering channels over time to promote the lowest possible delivered costs in the total flow of products from the manufacturer to the ultimate product user. To compete with companies like Dell Computer Corporation, which sold $546 million in mail-order computers in 1991, Digital Equipment in 1992 launched a $10-million marketing campaign to sell its personal computers by mail. Because mail-order is a higher-efficiency channel than such channels as personal computer dealers or direct selling, Digital Equipment is turning to it in order to greatly boost its sales on a product line in which prices are eroding (leaving less margin for Digital Equipment to afford more expensive marketing channel options!).[1]

While it is less disruptive for companies to try and assist traditional channels in remaining efficient and productive units over time, new channels in fact often start up on the single premise that they can move merchandise more efficiently. Superstores and price clubs are examples of new channels that are more efficient even than discounters. An industry study by McKinsey and Co. of warehouse clubs found they had a 26 percent average price advantage over supermarkets, half of which was from buying efficiencies (larger volume discounts) and the other half from operating efficiencies (higher labor productivity and lower facility costs). So despite a supplier's best efforts at working with its traditional resellers, it must often add to or switch away from its traditional channels to keep its sales up, as new efficiency channels emerge. Dell proved that mail order was a viable way of selling personal computers efficiently. Franchising has proven a more efficient channel for speedy oil changes than either car dealers or gasoline service stations. Price clubs proved that they could out-discount Kmart. Not all channels can sustain their vitality over time, as witnessed by the difficult time independent toy stores have had with the Toys R Us chain toy store leader. Toys R Us now sells more than 40 percent of all U.S. toys.

Astute Capacity Management

The successful management of channel capacity can take many forms, including adding channels in anticipation of burgeoning demand for the product, being more selective about channels, supplementing channel capacity through specialty distributors, and aiming for category dominance.

Adding Capacity

WD-40, the successful maker of all-purpose spray lubricants, moved its distribution channels from very specialized ones in its early years (such as gun shops, hobby stores, and specialty retailers of fishing reels and bikes) to mainstream hardware, discount, automotive, department, and even food- and drugstore channels. It added channel capacity using in-store sample sizes of its product to give away as trial packages. When people liked the product and returned to buy it, they often did so in channels that WD-40 had not traditionally been sold in.

L'Eggs pantyhose, a division of Sara Lee, was similarly astute in using novel egg-shaped packaging and floor displays to gain access to food- and drugstore channels to sell pantyhose, a product that prior to the L'Eggs onslaught sold only in department stores. So adding channel capacity in anticipation of demand is one way to continuously improve channel management.

Being Selective

A second variation is to be selective about channel capacity and to put more emphasis on selling more product overall through fewer total market outlets. In other words, some companies pick their spots, working with fewer but better channels. Tire manufacturers have done this by moving to distribute tires via automotive chains and specialists and placing less dependence on the corner service station as a distribution channel. Video producers are also becoming choosy about whom they will sell to and are cutting the total number of video distributors in favor of the major chains, which can out-merchandise the small mom-and-pop-type video rental stores.

In the United Kingdom, British Telecom is pruning its channel outlets for its cellular phone distribution because too many of the dealers it first set up were not "polished" in sales, image, or efficient phone installation and servicing. It hopes to do more business overall via a smaller number of dealers.

Supplementing Capacity

Yet a third way to manage capacity well is to supplement mainstream distribution channels with specialty distributors who cover selected market niches that are often overlooked by the larger channels. For instance, electrical products manufacturers sell most of their products through general-line electrical wholesalers such as Graybar Electric (of St. Louis, Missouri). But some also sell through additional channels that specialize in market niches such as lighting, security controls, factory automation, electric motors, and the like. 3M sells its occupational respirators through general-line safety supply distributors (who market everything from hard hats, gloves, and goggles to first-aid kits) and through specialty distributors serving welders, agricultural markets, and chemical markets, whose need for protection against hazards requires only a part of 3M's wide respirator line offering.

Going for Category Clout

A fourth way for companies to manage channel capacity is to try to stake out a large and dedicated part of their channels' shelf space, catalog space, or floor space. Frito-Lay does this in snack foods, bringing an enormous assortment to sustain the dedicated display space in their channels. These companies try to "own" a category so that no competitor can get into "their space." Stanley Tool does this in hardware, Black & Decker in power tools and housewares, Corning in cookware, Levi Strauss in casual denim apparel, Armstrong World Industries in floor tiling, and DuPont in pillows and sleep products. In effect, they try to maintain captive capacity and category clout, assuring their brands of dominance. Captive capacity dominance strategies succeed only if the company can over time sustain new products that keep its space "fresh" and "contemporary" in the eyes of the channel owners and ultimate consumers. If Frito-Lay did not keep innovating in snack foods with new flavors and assortments, it would not sustain its channel capacity. Likewise, Levi Strauss would not dominate channel shares in denim clothes if it stopped innovating. Soon its channel capacity would be eaten away by new rivals or by private label products of the retailer's own brand. In specialized retailers such as The Gap, this displacement of Levi's by The Gap's own jeans label has already occurred.

Knowing how much channel capacity to add as demand grows is not always easy. For instance, Osh Kosh B'Gosh is moving from high-priced department stores and specialty clothing stores into Sears and Penney's. The decision to add a chain such as J. C. Penney adds 1,400 more stores at one fell swoop. Will the $65 million in sales of Osh Kosh's bib overalls that Penney is expected to generate merely cannibalize Osh Kosh's other channels, or will it represent *added* sales volume? Osh Kosh is betting that it will reach new customers, who don't now buy kids' overalls at Bloomingdale's, Saks, or Marshall Field. This is a difficult gamble in that the loss of some big upscale chains could offset the brand's extra sales via midpriced chains and possibly depress the brand's image as well, causing a loss of pricing punch (the ability to get its full list prices and avoid markdowns).[2]

Tulsa General Insurance has installed NCR 5682 computer terminals in local supermarkets to allow drivers to apply for its automobile insurance electronically. Prospects get rate quotes and temporary policies, which are later firmed up and mailed to customers by the company's headquarters in Tulsa. Tulsa General is adding channel capacity to boost sales. Whether Tulsa succeeds depends on its ability to tap new insurance prospects via a novel location and sales method.

One company that has very successfully managed its channel capacity is Gatorade. Begun as a specialized sports drink, Gatorade was originally sold to sports teams, gyms, and fitness clubs. Then mainstream supermarket channels were added, followed by convenience 7-11–type stores and selected drug stores. Now Gatorade can be found in vending machines and even in fast food minirestaurants in malls. As channel capacity has increased, Gatorade has moved from a specialty isotonic beverage for athletes to a mass-marketed brand, increasingly as available as everyday beverages such as milk, pop, or juice. Gatorade's sales exceed hundreds of millions of dollars per year in North America, and it has more than 92 percent of its niche market.

Boosting Channel Yield: The "Pull" Factor

There's an old expression that you can lead a horse to water, but you can't make him drink. The same holds true of channel management. Getting channels set up helps only if the product or service can sustain its sales *through* the channel. For instance, Sony's Beta videotapes, the first to reach the market, originally had exposure in thousands of retail cassette rental outlets. But Sony could not sustain its place in the channel because VHS taping systems gained more popularity with customers, and stores had to maintain VHS tape inventories as well as Sony's Beta tapes. This dual inventorying of tapes was very expensive for store owners, and as Sony's initial popularity began to wane, channels had to choose to carry either a limited inventory of Beta *and* VHS tapes or a full selection of VHS and a proportionately smaller Beta section. The channels opted for the latter strategy, effectively abandoning Sony's format. As more video stores adopted this strategy, consumers found Beta tapes ever harder to rent, and, as the market for hardware evolved from renting VCRs to owning them, they turned to buying more VHS systems. This of course made the all-VHS tape inventory strategy even more viable for channels, so the cycle fed upon itself. Thus, while channel capacity initially was not a problem at all for Sony, as its yield per retailer fell, it eventually lost its capacity market coverage via the retailers as well.

Boosting yield from a channel is very much a function of whether the manufacturer creates demand for its products at the end-customer level so that the channel's sales remain healthy and its asset turnover high; it also involves assisting the channel's own capabilities of selling its products. In retail channels, boosting ultimate customer demand usually means advertising to create brand preference, thus drawing willing customers to the retailer for the product. Two excellent examples of companies that have done well are DuPont, with its Stainmaster carpet, and Gillette, with its Sensor brand razor and shaving system. Each heavily advertised the brand's attributes and drew customers to retail channels to purchase it. Gillette spent $80 million in one year to advertise Sensor globally. Sensor and Stainmaster have made many retailers very happy because of the brisk demand for these brands.

This is a classic example of consumer "pull." In commercial, business-to-business markets, demand pull is more often than not a function of sales force end-user call activity aimed at pulling the manufacturer's products through the distributor's or dealer's operation. Chemical companies do this when they send out highly trained engineer/sales representatives to call on chemical customers whose orders are then placed ultimately with chemical product distributors.

Satisfactory channel yield is almost impossible without some form of pull on the channel. As packaged-goods producers cut back their "pull" branded advertising in favor of very costly short-term deals with retailers, the retailers' "own" store brands are selling better. Any channel yield equation that ignores the need for sustained end-customer pull activities is doomed to suboptimization. That is why, despite decades of ad exposure by Maytag of its "loneliest repairman," it still continues to spend for such commercials. Its appliance share and sales by dealer are greatly affected by the customer's belief in Maytag's product superiority and durability—in other words, in its brand equity.

Boosting Channel Yield: The "Support" Factor

The other part of channel yield involves astutely supporting dealers or distributors so that they can add to "pull" with their own marketing, promoting, selling, or servicing efforts. A dealer's own floor sales rep or the Maytag dealership can also affect Maytag's business by virtue of salesmanship, negotiating on price, promises and arrangements on appliance delivery, financing options, and guarantees on service after sale (should the appliance need any repair).

As the manufacturer, Maytag can provide dealers with assistance to help train sales and service personnel; dealership financing packages; and help for underwriting some of the dealership's local ad costs via co-op ad allowances or directed promotions. What separates outstanding marketing from mediocre marketing among manufacturers using channels of distribution is the imagination shown in designing channel supports and the proficiency displayed in executing them over time.

Figure 6-2 lists the variety of service supports for distributors that can be provided by manufacturers. The type of support will vary according to whether the company's intention is to boost the distributor's financial, technical, logistical, sales, or marketing core capabilities.

Manufacturers who weave a web of supports often create enduring distributor partnerships. For instance, in 1939, Gates Rubber of Denver set up a distributor in Grand Island, Nebraska — the Kelly Supply Co. — to sell V-Belts and hydraulic hose couplings. Gates offers a broad array of creative supports, including the best returned-goods policies and warranties in the industry. Semiannually, Gates allows its distributors to return slow-moving stock and replace it with fast-moving items on a dollar-for-dollar basis, with no upper limit on the amount. Gates is the only one of 700 suppliers selling via Kelly that has a single customer service person assigned to handle *all* aspects of Kelly's account. Therefore, Kelly need not waste time calling different parts of the Gates Rubber organization to find out about shipping, billing, product availability, or pricing, because Gates offers a one-contact service person to save Kelly this kind of annoyance. In return for such dedicated support, Kelly, in more than fifty years of operating, has never carried or sold products that compete with the Gates line of V-Belts and rubber products.[3]

Supplier supports to retailers often take the form of computer-to-computer hookups, which transfer data on orders, sales, and the like so that the suppliers can provide accurate just-in-time service.

Levi Strauss, for instance, uses its Levilink, an electronic data interchange system, so that when a pair of jeans is sold at one of its retailers, the information goes directly to Levi Strauss, where it automatically generates a re-order, invoice, and packing slip. Logistical supports are also a common element in boosting yield via retail channels. For instance the Gitano Group, the fashion manufacturer, invested time in studying the store receiving system of its retail customer Wal-Mart. It discovered that if it shipped its clothing already prehung on hangers, instead of packed in boxes, it could help Wal-Mart cycle its inventory to store displays one day sooner. This cut Wal-Mart's handling costs 5 percent, at minimal cost to Gitano. Wal-Mart in turn passed this saving on to its customers by offering prices that were lower by 5 percent, and Gitano's sales were given an added boost.

Distributor supports (such as those listed in Figure 6-2) often have quite varied effects on a distributor's working capital requirements, expenses, asset turnover, and revenues. For instance, when a manufacturer provides better margins on slower turnover lines, this helps offset the distributor's working capital needs, since slow movers always remain longer in inventory, thus costing money before they are sold.

Supports such as special freight or advertising allowances directly offset the expenses a distributor would otherwise incur in the conduct of its business. Supports such as joint sales calls, in which the manufacturer's sales force works with the distributor's reps, can boost the distributor's revenue from otherwise more-difficult-to-sell large target accounts, where such assistance makes a difference. Providing a distributor's sales force with sufficient samples of new products is another support that can induce new product trials and repeat purchases by the distributor's customers. Almost any support can be gauged as to its positive effects on either the productivity of the distributor's operations (management of sales expenses and margins) or the productivity of its assets (inventories, receivables, warehouses, fleets, computer systems, or other current or fixed assets).

As a company sells to more than one type of channel, its supports must often be customized to each channel's specific needs. For example, 3M sells it Scotch brand line of household tapes and

(*text continues on page 108*)

Figure 6-2. Manufacturer's service supports for distributors, by functional area.

Communications	Sales Force	Technical	Logistics	Pricing	Promotional	Financial	General
Distributor councils	Target account programs	Technical reps	Minimum order quantities	Volume discounts (by order)	Free goods	Leasing plans	Territory protection
Dinner meetings	Joint sales calls	Technical training	24-hour delivery	Year-end rebates	Off-invoice allowances	Floor stock	Brand advertising
Joint-association work	Joint trade shows	Catalog simplification	Drop-shipping	Special allowances	Introductory offers	Consignment stock	Patents, trademarks
Electronic mail nets	Training, demonstrations, clinics	1-800 hot lines	Fast order turnaround	Return privileges	Contests	Equipment on loan	Emphasis on quality
Newsletters	Plant tours	Technical manuals	Expediting	Prepaid freight	Customized direct mail		Stream of new products

Mobile vans	Recognition clubs	Allowing order add-ons	Low surcharge for custom orders	Sales aids	Innovativeness
Staff exchanges	Sharing success stories			Premiums	Second brands for low-price markets
Joint market surveys				Samples	
				Coupons	
				Point-of-purchase materials	
				Catalogs	
				Cooperative advertising	
				Lead exchanges	

Source: Reprinted by permission of the publisher from "Manufacturers' Services for Distributors," by Allan J. Magrath and Kenneth G. Hardy, *Industrial Marketing Management Journal*, Vol. 21, No. 2 (May 1992), pp. 119–124. Copyright © 1992 by Elsevier Science Publishing Co., Inc.

dispensers to drug chains, department stores, price clubs, discount stores (such as Kmart), gift shops, hardware stores, variety stores, convenience stores, toy stores, card shops, and numerous other retail channels. Supports for some of these channels emphasize bulk displays with simple assortments, while others emphasize racks or shelf displays of varied size assortments. Some in-store merchandise supports from 3M are upscale (for card or gift shops), while others are very basic; some are much larger than others in accordance with the differing store sizes and floor space available. So in trying to maximize yield from multiple channels, it is vital to customize supports to meet differing channel conditions and marketing interests. Trade class complexity is a fact of life for manufacturers producing wide-spectrum-use consumer goods. Duracell's president and CEO has attributed a large measure of his company's success in marketing batteries to its skill at matching channel supports with the vast and complex network of different retail channels to which it markets. With small batteries in use for cellular phones, camcorders, cameras, pocket calculators, small computers, pagers, toys, garage door openers, flashlights, security systems, Walkman radios, and thousands of other applications, Duracell has had to master multiple channel support offerings on a global basis.[4]

Channel supports are a little like computer software, while channel capacity parallels computer hardware. All the hardware capacity in the world is quite worthless without the right operating software to make it work. Both capacity and supports are needed for channel success, yet each must be individually managed for excellence.

Leveraging Channel Yields via Channelwide Training and Communications

Boosting yield via distributors, dealers, or other channels isn't only a matter of custom-tailoring decisions to individual distributors. Industrywide initiatives also pay off. In one major study of what motivates middlemen, it was found that the second-most effective motivator, after appealing financial inducements (such as volume discounts or other dollar incentives), was effective communication vehicles whereby distributors could talk with manufacturers about their problems and concerns.[5] Dayco Corporation, a manufacturer of engineered plastic and rubber products, uses a distributor council to boost its overall distributor yield. At intensive four-day advisory council meetings, Dayco lets a selection of its top distributors discuss what they think of Dayco's marketing programs, sales policies, credit policies, new products, and any other issues the distributors consider critical. Dayco implements 75 percent of the distributor proposals for improvements.[6]

Close to a fifth of all U.S. electrical manufacturers employ distributor councils to gain feedback and improvement suggestions for their operating policies and tactics, in such areas as returned goods, promised promotions, incentive plans, approaches to new markets, and other areas often covered by formal distributor agreements.

Specialized Bicycle Components of California held roundtable discussions with fifteen of its top bike dealers to determine their advance reaction to Specialized's proposed 1992 mountain bike designs. Each of the fifteen key dealers' sales staffs rated bikes as to the appeal of their features, colors, and overall "design look." These dealer advisory roundtables led Specialized to winnow its forty designs down to the best twenty-six. Although Specialized spent $800 for each of the dealer roundtables, it saved $100,000 in further product development costs and millions in inventory investments.[7] So dealers can be useful as sounding boards on new products as well as on ongoing marketing or sales policy issues.

Disney uses an advisory board of travel agents to keep in touch with how it can help these agents boost the sales of Disney tour packages. It has used this advisory board to boost its educational tools for "easy" agent reference to Disney's four resorts—in Anaheim, California; Lake Buena Vista, Florida; Tokyo; and France. More than 800 travel agents have attended some of Disney's advisory board meetings over the years since 1982.

McDonald's uses a formal training school (its so-called Hamburger University) for its franchisees to help boost channel yield.

Compaq Computer trains its dealers in regional centers, certifying them in the sale of its more advanced computers. In fact, when Compaq launched its advanced System-Pro line of file servers in 1989, it trained 8,300 dealer personnel in seventeen U.S.

cities, using thirty-four trainers in a six-month blitz (from late 1989 to spring 1990). Its dealers have sold more than 10,000 units since it began this training effort.

Channel Efficiency

So far, discussion has centered on leveraging channel capacity and boosting channel yield. The former focuses on market coverage challenges, the latter on output tactics. Adding channel capacity at just the right time or cleverly supporting channels in just the right way can both work to boost the channel system's overall performance. Ultimately, however, the delegation of functions and costs among all parts of the distribution channel system determines its efficiency.

Thus manufacturers can also look to basic channel functions to search for new ways to improve efficiency that go beyond merely changing the mix, type, or density of distribution (capacity) or getting output higher per dealer/wholesaler/retailer.

Three types of strategies are commonly utilized to improve a channel system's efficiency. The first involves redesigning the channel to bypass middlemen entirely; the second involves subcontracting functions out; and the third, using another company's distribution system.

Bypassing the Middleman

Baxter International, the supplier of health care, bypasses pharmacies by delivering its prescriptions directly to Health Maintenance Organizations (HMOs), corporations, and union customers. Its efficiency has assisted it in growing this part of its business from nearly zero in 1985 to close to $1 billion in 1992.

20th Century Industries, a California-based auto and home insurer, sells policies by telephone directly to consumers, bypassing agents (who are the usual channel for this type of insurance). 20th Century thereby saves 15 percent in commissions and yet incurs only one percent in direct teleselling costs. This strategy has made 20th Century the most efficient insurer in all of California, and enables it to provide the lowest insurance rates as well. Its profitable return on equity for shareholders exceeded 30 percent in 1991.[8] So improving channel efficiency usually boosts financial indices for a company. Wal-mart, for its part, requires its suppliers to bypass manufacturer rep channels and deal with it directly as a way of keeping its lead in retailing efficiency.

Subcontracting Functions

A second method often employed to enhance efficiency is to subcontract functions usually performed by one part of the system to a more efficient provider.

When retailers band together to form a buying group entity, they subcontract to this entity the task of efficiently buying from suppliers at larger discounts. Often manufacturers will subcontract service on their hardware or equipment to third parties, who can provide faster and less expensive service to customers than can the manufacturers themselves or even the manufacturers' appointed distributors.

This third-party servicing efficiency becomes possible because such third parties are specialists who are not required, as the distributors are, to display, sell, and assort the manufacturers' lines. As specialists, third parties become very expert in the management of repair shops, tools, technicians, test or diagnostic equipment, spare parts, and repair scheduling.

Piggybacking Others' Efficiency

Yet a third way of improving a channel's efficiency is to go to market entirely by piggybacking, or using, another company's distribution system. IBM is marketing its Notebook computers in Japan this way by way of Hitachi. Hitachi will buy 2,000 of IBM's computers per month and sell them for IBM under the Hitachi brand name. IBM hopes to find in Hitachi a more efficient method for getting its personal computer operating systems into the hands of more Japanese customers. Robert Bosch GmbH is marketing its heavy industrial tools (jigsaws, rotary hammers) in a joint venture using Emerson Electric's U.S. distributors, which market companion-type products under the Skil brand name (circular saws and electrical power tools). Syntex, a pharmaceutical manufacturer

Figure 6-3. Boosting channel system yield.

✓ Add multiple channels as demand expands.

✓ Prune marginal performers within selected channels.

✓ Use a matrix of general-line channels overlayed with specialized channels to cover every possible market niche.

✓ Try to dominate your product category in the chosen channel.

✓ Use a mix of consumer pull tactics and trade supports to motivate channels, build their capabilities, and attract end consumers.

✓ Piggyback other companies' established channels.

✓ Subcontract different channel functions to middlemen for optimum efficiency.

✓ Bypass channels where no efficient alternative is possible.

---

with experience only in the marketing of prescription drugs, will partner with Procter & Gamble to sell its over-the-counter version of its popular Naprosyne drug.

The Relativity of Efficiency

Boosting channel efficiency is never a clear-cut decision. For instance, Alloy Rods Corporation and Lincoln Electric Company both manufacture and sell welding rod electrodes to contractors, steel fabricators, and other industrial buyers in the United States. But Alloy Rods sells 87 percent of its electrodes via wholesalers or distributors, whereas Lincoln sells 40 percent of its product through distributors, and 60 percent direct. Alloy's market share and margins are considerably lower than Lincoln's, so it finds the use of more distribution the only cost-effective way to get to market. Its constrained financial condition forces it to invest less in direct selling than Lincoln can afford.

Lincoln's use of direct selling is efficient as evidenced by its superior margins and leading industry share of market. So both these companies can be said to be using efficient channels as measured against their constraints and results, even though the two companies have very different efficiency strategies.[9]

Ultimately, maximum channel efficiency means finding the distribution method that offers the lowest delivered cost so as to benefit end-user customers (in lower prices) and provide the leverage for market gains in share versus less efficient rivals. 3M's better channel efficiency in the sale and delivery of its Post-it Notes via office stationers forced Avery Dennison to abandon its challenge to 3M in this business.

Figure 6-3 summarizes the key ways of boosting channel yield through process improvement.

Notes

1. John Schneidawind, "DEC Plans to Sell PC's by Mail," *U.S.A. Today* (January 13, 1992), section B, p. 1.

2. Julia Siler and Stephanie Forest, "Osh Kosh B'Gosh May Be Risking Its Upscale Image," *Business Week* (July 15, 1991), p. 140.

3. Christine Forbes, "50 Years and Counting," *Industrial Distribution* (December 1991), pp. 49–50.

4. Joyce Oliver, "Duracell CEO Charged Up About His Company," *Marketing News* (November 11, 1991), p. 2.

5. David D. Shipley, "Selection and Motivation of Distribution Intermediaries," *Industrial Marketing Management Journal*, Vol. 13 (1984), pp. 249–256.

6. James Narus and James Anderson, "Turn Your Industrial Distributors Into Partners," *Harvard Business Review* (March–April 1986), p. 68.

7. Susan Greco, "Making Customer Roundtables Work," *Inc.* magazine (February 1992), pp. 99–100.

8. "To Hell with Efficiency," *Forbes* (January 6, 1992), p. 163.

9. For a complete write-up of this efficiency strategy contrast, see Frank V. Cespedes, "Control versus Resources in Channel Design: Distribution Differences in One Industry," *Industrial Marketing Management Journal*, Vol. 17 (1988), pp. 215–227.

7

The Logistics and Customer Service System

When something goes awry, the customer's sense of frustration with service is very high, and expectations for a quick or easy resolution of the problem are likely low. In short, the conditions are ripe to "knock the customer's socks off" with excellent service . . . to exceed customers' expectations.

Professor Leonard Berry
Texas A&M University

One survey by the University of Florida on why customers select vendors showed that over half the reasons cited were related to logistics.[1] Elements such as meeting promised delivery dates, accuracy in filling orders, advance notice of shipping delays, and quick action on complaints all rated as more important than product quality, product features, or price factors. The reason? A late or inaccurate product delivery can cost a customer more than the actual product cost, so service quality defect costs often exceed product quality defect costs. Conversely, improving the process of handling customer service can greatly boost a company's overall reputation for quality together with its business results.

Wal-Mart's superior logistics ensures that its 1,700 stores get all the goods they need on time via twenty highly automated warehouses and a communications network that ties store inventories back to key suppliers (such as Gitano) and to the supplier's supplier (Gitano's fabric supplier for its jeans). The result of superior customer service is reflected in Wal-Mart's growth and profits, which far surpass those of Sears, J. C. Penney, Kmart, and regional retailers such as Ames, Dayton-Hudson, and Caldor. While the five-year average of its competitors' return on equity was 13.7 percent, Wal-Mart's was 35 percent (1987–1992), and it outgrew the five-year average sales growth of its rivals by a factor of almost three times (30.3 percent per year for Wal-Mart versus 11.5 percent for its competitors).[2] Wal-Mart's logistics expertise has been so superb that it has helped the company in its ability to branch out into other retail formats, such as its "Sam's Club"—a wholesale membership chain.

In the shoe industry, Nike is considered head and shoulders above the rest in logistics performance. Its "Nike Next Day" guarantee ensures that merchant store orders will be filled and delivered within twenty-four hours. This is despite Nike's 800 shoe models for twenty-five different sports. In industrial marketing, logistics is just as key in conferring advantage on a manufacturer. For instance, when 324 participating office furniture dealers were asked in a national study to select the most important factors (from a list of twenty-four different factors) that they used to choose from among 200 different vendors, three of the top seven factors they listed were logistics factors, namely, meeting promised delivery dates, using advanced ordering methods, and vendor accuracy in forecasting to contract project orders.[3] Among the other twenty-four factors were competitiveness of pricing, finished product quality, breadth of product offering, and the adequacy of promotional materials.

What Comprises a Logistics and Customer Service System?

A logistics and customer service system in those areas specifically related to marketing involves three major operations (as shown in Figure 7-1): (1) the front-end order handling and customer service functions; (2) the order fulfillment subsystem, including finished goods warehousing, inventory management, outbound transportation, expediting, and the paperwork flow/documentation accompanying these functions; and (3) order follow-up and customer service measurement to ensure that customers are proactively re-

Figure 7-1. A conceptual overview of the marketing logistics and customer service system.

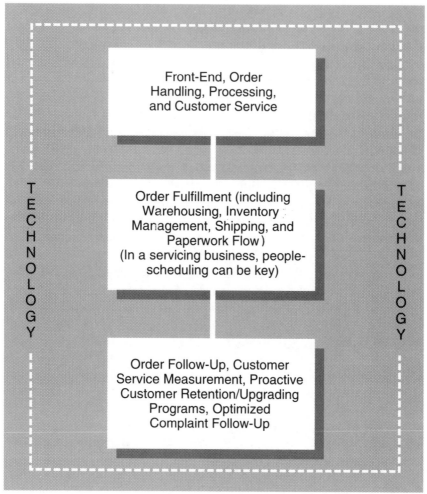

tained, optimally satisfied, and, wherever possible, given value-added services that encourage even higher repurchase rates.

Tying each of these operations together is technology, applied to the three processes to give them integrity, efficiency, and effectiveness. For instance, information system technology may assist in rapid order processing or in customer service personnel knowing order status information in "real time" on an account's buying profile and order history. Technology in warehousing could involve bar code scanners and automated material handling, while transportation could involve computer-assisted route planning for shipping, expediting systems, backhauling optimization, and advanced tracking systems. Order follow-up may use the technology of tele-selling or data base management for customer mailings, complaint follow-ups, or order upgrade programs.

Logistics that relate to factory materials management, purchasing activities, or inbound transportation of raw materials to the factory are not included as part of the logistics system related to marketing. That is because these components of *total* logistics are concerned with the factory as the customer rather than with the ultimate user-customer. In fact, supplier qualification and certification programs are "reverse marketing," an attempt to connect with vendors in partnerships as astutely and tightly as with customers.

The System Dynamics That Count Most in Logistics and Customer Service Areas

Logistics in the marketing field focuses on three key system outputs and three system characteristics. Outputs that count include responsiveness or speed in order handling and fulfillment; lowest possible delivered costs for products or services (in the customers' eyes); and minimal waste in the system (such as inventory holding in various locations, which ties up scarce working capital). Low delivered costs are always relative to the customer's value perception. So while the logistics system at Toyota strives for low delivered costs in auto deliveries and customer service, the relevant target for such savings is Toyota's target customer. Clearly such costs may differ substantially from the low-delivered-cost perceptions of Mercedes-Benz customers. Customer segments determine value perceptions and drive cost standards. First-class airline passengers and economy passengers, for instance, have entirely different value expectations about the services they are to receive.

System characteristics routinely targeted for continuous improvement are capacity (to handle demand under a variety of conditions), proficiency (to guarantee right-the-first-time shipping or invoicing), and efficiency related to minimizing the handling of paperwork or products. For instance, minimizing product handling involves the optimized design of warehouse layouts to cut the distances traveled by goods inside the warehouse. Scheduling just-in-time supplies greatly improves efficiency.

Because Caterpillar Tractor suppliers deliver just-in-time, the company can in turn guarantee Caterpillar dealers 99.72 percent on-time delivery of parts, within its targeted seventy-two–hour part delivery promise.

In retailing or banking, optimized service fulfillment systems often involve automation, self-service, and specialized layout designs that minimize customer waiting.

In the airline business, where delayed passengers can hold up take-offs and cost money, new technology is being used to service customers better while saving the airlines costs. British Airways is using new technology that allows it to comb lineups at Heathrow Airport for late-arriving passengers. It is also using hand-held computers (that transmit on a radio frequency) to check in these passengers and tag their luggage on the spot, allowing fuller planes to depart on time. These computers have access to the mainframe reservation system. British Airways will potentially save $16 million in fuel, since a one-minute departure delay uses $1,800 worth of jet fuel.

Front-End Customer Service

Companies considered excellent in logistics, as related to marketing, frequently do a superb job of front-end customer handling. Figure 7-2 lists some of these noteworthy companies. To continuously improve their customer service front-end tasks and functions, these fine companies embrace four concepts and practices.

Or Your Money Back

First, their top managements are committed to the philosophy that the customer counts most, and they often put their beliefs into specific promised performance terms. For example, Caterpillar Tractor promises to deliver spare parts to any of its worldwide customers within seventy-two hours. Domino's pledges to deliver its

Figure 7-2. Companies demonstrating excellence in logistics service.

Manufacturers	Service Companies	Retailers
General Electric	Four Seasons Hotels	L. L. Bean
Xerox	Marriott	Nordstrom's
IBM	Federal Express	Marks & Spencer (U.K.)
Caterpillar	American Express	IKEA (Sweden)
Rubbermaid	Domino's Pizza	
Daimler Benz	McDonald's	
Apple Computer	USAA (insurance and investment management company)	

pizza within thirty minutes or the customer doesn't have to pay. Xerox gives a lifetime warranty on its equipment, pledging that Xerox will provide 100 percent satisfaction to its customers or they can return their equipment. L. L. Bean returns your money if its products are defective, often years after the product was purchased.

Communicating With the Customer

Second, these companies invest heavily in communication and order handling systems to save their customers time, money, and inconvenience in getting orders processed, questions answered, or needs met. Such system investments are often designed to accommodate both routine and emergency customer service requests. Examples include 800-number ordering service lines, fax networks, or electronic data interchange systems in which a customer can hook up its computer to the vendor's computer to exchange ordering, invoicing, and other information. General Electric's answer center logs three million calls a year from customers, a third of which are related to service issues, a third to product operation issues, and a third to general inquiries about products (prices, retail availabilities, and so on). Obviously, one part of continuous improvement in front-end customer service is to make it as easy as possible for customers to reach you.

Getting Customer Feedback

Yet a third element of optimum customer service involves having a continuous feedback loop from customers from a diverse set of "listening" posts. Many leading companies employ a half dozen types of listening, including formal customer surveys (Xerox surveys 40,000 customers per month); customer roundtable forums; the analysis of complaint reports or field sales reports from sales reps; customer comment cards packed in with merchandise (or, as restaurants/hotels do, placed in rooms or on dining tables); end-user clubs (of, say, Apple Macintosh personal computer users); and focus groups or distributor councils.[4] Figure 7-3 lists these major listening posts.

Figure 7-3. Customer feedback listening posts concerning service.

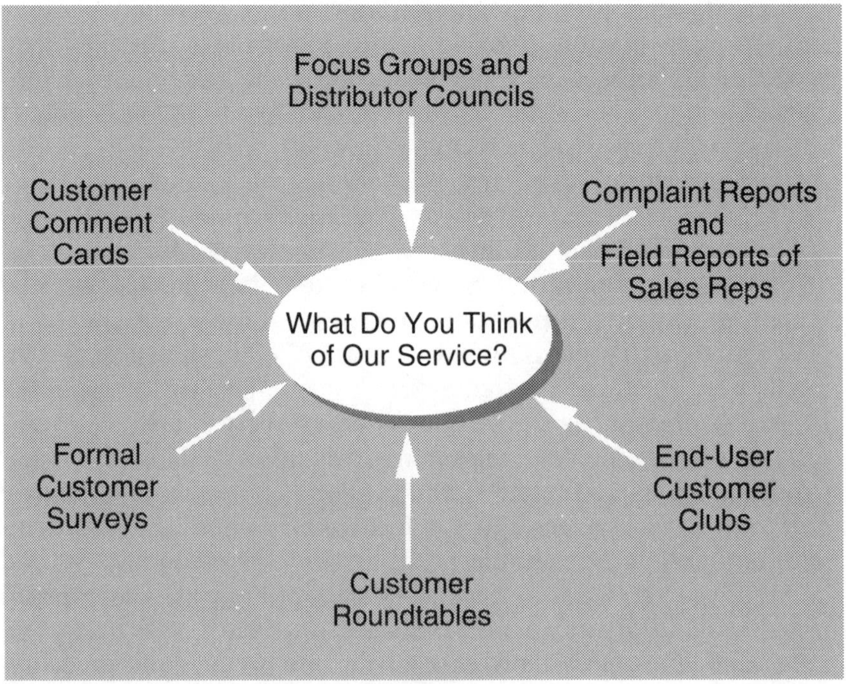

Focus Groups and
Distributor Councils

Customer
Comment
Cards

Complaint Reports
and
Field Reports of
Sales Reps

What Do You Think
of Our Service?

Formal
Customer
Surveys

End-User
Customer
Clubs

Customer
Roundtables

Techsonic Industries of Eufaula, Alabama, for example, conducts focus groups of sports fishermen and uses their comments to fine-tune its services and "depth-finding" product lines. Companies such as Rubbermaid demand that their operating personnel visit customers' premises and listen to their needs and suggestions. At Four Seasons Hotels, executives in the senior management tier must serve as general manager in each of the hotels they oversee to stay in touch with the hotel-using customers. This kind of customer listening has resulted in repeat guest rates at Four Seasons that exceed 70 percent occupancy (one of the highest ratios for the industry).

Training Employees in Customer Service

A fourth part of excellent front-end customer service involves instilling company personnel with friendly, helpful attitudes and training them in the practices that ensure first-rate customer service. Such practices embrace seven key principles: (1) hiring capable and customer-friendly personnel; (2) providing all employees with lots of training courses on customer handling; (3) empowering employees through delegation of authority to keep customers content; (4) providing incentives for employees who demonstrate dedicated service to customers; (5) providing recognition for excellent customer servers; (6) putting customer service teams in place wherever teamwork works better than individualized service; and (7) continually measuring customer service dimensions that customers say count with them. Figure 7-4 illustrates these principles in graphic form.

Clearly, insofar as customers are concerned, it is the front-line employee who often determines what the customer feels about a company's service. For instance, the Four Seasons clerk who greets you at the check-in desk counts for far more than the hotel's manager. Similarly, a customer is less impressed by the 600,000 packages handled at Federal Express's Memphis hub than by how the Federal Express courier handled his own package that day.

Recruitment. Personnel practices start with hiring. General Electric hires Spanish- and French-speaking operators to man its 800-number service lines for Puerto Rico, South America, and

Figure 7-4. Focused personnel practices for customer-service excellence.

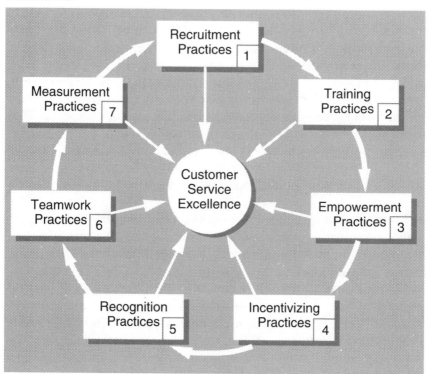

Canada, where French-speaking Quebequers represent close to a third of the country. Four Seasons recruitment screening is the toughest in the hotel industry. At Franklin International Institute in Salt Lake City, customer service reps are hired on the basis of criteria that go beyond the requirement of a college education to consider a potential employee's life experience, ethics, and level of personal integrity.

At Aetna Life Insurance, new hires are screened for their "customer focus mentality" by exploring, in interviews and tests, the candidate's responses to customer service case situations, assessing the candidate's understanding of what customer service excellence means, and gauging how well past experience has prepared the potential employee for focusing on the customer (versus focusing on the task).

Training. Training in service excellence is the next critical variable. At Sky Dome, Toronto's huge stadium (where the Toronto Blue Jays play), 180 full-time and 500 part-time staff host 68,000 people literally every operating night, 320-plus nights a year. Each part-time or full-time staffer gets twenty to twenty-five hours, respectively, of intensive training in customer service so that they can handle anything from finding a lost child to repairing a broken seat or arranging emergency first aid.[5] Part of Aetna Life's key training for employees is a ten-day course on defined competencies, one of which is customer focus.

Empowerment. Empowerment for customer service employees means transferring to front-line service people genuine authority (and management backup) to satisfy customers in whatever way works—without first having to refer to company policy manuals or supervisors. For example, 3M sales reps can issue instant credit to a customer for merchandise that the customer wants to return for credit. This allows customers to get instant service, as opposed to waiting for long bureaucratic approval processes that occur when the head office gets involved.

Typical company training programs that emphasize customer service teach problem solving, listening, communication, and stress management skills.[6] Companies committed to empowerment also tend to publicize and praise employee efforts in this direction and often try to make role models out of such individuals for others to emulate. Service excellence without empowerment is seldom possible because customers usually wind up getting satisfaction only by dealing with management personnel, the only ones with the authority necessary to act in satisfying them.

Empowerment is often more rhetoric than reality, however, because managers who empower others to act on their behalf often do so only with those they can second-guess or trust not to make mistakes that will embarrass them. True empowerment is a transfer of power, and it does involve risk because mistakes will often occur. Risks can be mitigated with training, knowledgeable employees, and communication, but they remain risks nonetheless.

Incentivizing Practices. Incentivizing service excellence usually involves widening and deepening the pool of incentives normally used for service excellence, such as trips or extra pay for good performance. Some companies favor point systems in which points are awarded for customer service performance—points that can then be cashed in for prizes ranging from gift certificates to specific awards.

Aetna Life Insurance incentivizes its service employees to strive for the mastery of six service goals: speed, accuracy, promptness, accessibility, caring, and quality staffing. Those employees exemplifying these performance goals attend a huge customer service celebration gala at which major prizes are presented, including the grand prize of an all-expenses-paid trip for two to Monte Carlo, Monaco.[7]

Recognizing Excellence. Recognition is another key building block in seeing to it that the spotlight remains fixed on improving service. At Aetna, semiannual president's breakfasts recognize fifteen to twenty employees who come to discuss service quality with the CEO. Recognition programs underline the old adage that most of us will never do great things but that we can all do small things in a great way. And, given this, recognition underscores how much value the company places on such customer-focused accomplishments.

Teamwork. Teamwork is crucial to a great deal of customer service because customer concerns often can't be dealt with by individual effort alone. For instance, a major study of why car-buying customers switch away from dealerships showed that 68 percent do so because of the dealer's sales or service personnel's indifference, while only 14 percent switch because of dissatisfaction with the car.[8] Clearly, automotive manufacturers can never optimize customer service without the full pledge and teamwork involvement of their dealers.

Amoco is moving to a teamwork organization and dismantling its functional hierarchies because multidisciplined teams can move faster and solve problems more decisively.

When ITT Sheraton reorganized its hotels in an attempt to run on a teamwork basis (where customer needs defined priorities), it was able to cut its management base from 40 to 14 (per hotel) and its employee base from 200 to 140 (per hotel), while *boosting* customer satisfaction among its 300 suite customers (again, per hotel).

Measuring Practices. Measurement underpins all continuous improvement efforts in customer service because, without it, the mix of speed and quality required to delight customers can't be ascertained. And wrongful measurement can be worse than no measurement. For instance, GTE spent $170,000 to train its telephone service personnel to "own" the customer's problem and to emphasize service over speed. But the measurements used in performance reviews of these same people emphasized low time per call, effectively contradicting GTE's own training imperatives. Domino's Pizza uses external customer service measurements to measure store service, and internal measurements in which stores rate Domino's distribution company on its order turnaround time and the quality of the pizza ingredients received at the stores. Its external measures of stores are accomplished by Domino's paying $60 each to "mystery" customers to buy pizzas throughout the year at its 5,000 locations and then evaluate the delivery and pizza quality upon delivery. The compensation of store managers and key employees is tied to these mystery customer ratings.[9]

Any genuine effort to boost the quality of a logistics and customer service system's front-end service must include an integrated approach to employee commitment, training, recognition, teamwork, rewards, and measurement of service excellence.

Order Fulfillment

As Figure 7-1 illustrates, fulfilling orders also has a big effect on quality. Being friendly, focused, and fast at taking orders all goes for naught if order fulfillment is slow or sloppy. Often it is technology that provides for order fulfillment efficiency, proficiency, and capacity. For example, Mrs. Field's Cookies, using customized software and a personal computer network tied into its individual stores, helps store managers schedule staffing, order raw material batches, and forecast sales by day so that they can concentrate on having just the right cookies and clerks on hand for customer service.

Valley National Bank of Arizona uses technology in order fulfillment on personal loans. Its lending process connects branch personal computers to the mainframe at headquarters, and by inputting customer data from the branch (from personal-loan officers), the system can access the customer's head office file, get a credit bureau check in "real time," and not only transmit the approval electronically, but also arrange the printed loan documentation for the customer to sign on the spot at the local branch.[10]

These kinds of order fulfillment systems demonstrate a balance between what has been called high tech and high touch, a combination of technology and personal service that results in speed, accuracy, and the personal touch—in this case, offered by Valley's personal-loan officers.

Frequently, in order to understand how to boost order fulfillment quality, a company must flowchart the sequence of processes used in its order fulfillment. By doing this so-called blueprinting, a company can figure out where its "fail points" (where deficiencies are most likely to occur) or bottlenecks are, whether these are in the warehousing system or shipping/transportation system (for products) or some other process area for a service organization. Simply automating a current system that is poorly designed by using high-speed technology is akin to paving a cowpath.

Arby's is cooperating with MasterCard to make it possible for patrons to buy fast-food meals in its restaurants on credit, in the past considered virtually a contradiction in terms. With new technology offered by MasterCard, fast credit approval is possible at the fast food counter by swiping the credit card through a checkout reader that hooks by satellite broadcast to MasterCard's headquarters.

Banks, by blueprinting such operations as bill paying, loan applications, cash withdrawals, and currency counting by tellers, have automated many of these services. Automated teller machines (ATMs) are now used routinely to pay bills and withdraw cash. Cash adapting machines eliminate teller cash counting. In some cases, banks are moving their services out to their customers. For example, safety deposit box services are being offered at nursing homes, and, to improve order fulfillment in congested downtown parking areas, banks are providing shuttle services to better parking facilities.

This blueprinting allows delays or congestion to be identified, after which new solutions can be considered to sort them out. For instance, in hotel operations blueprinting, order fulfillment is slowed by lineups at check-in counters, so now many hotels pre-register guests, who on arrival need only pick up their key and go to their room. Or the hotel may operate a registration desk at the airport so that guests can avoid lining up at the hotel and proceed directly to their rooms on arrival. Likewise, price-checking technology has been loaded into supermarket and department store cash registers to speed up customer checkouts.

Technology can boost capacity as well as speed. For instance, at USAA, a major property and casualty insurer, an optical disc and scanning system allows twenty-five million documents to be digitized, stored, sorted, and retrieved so that policy service reps can instantly call up, on their computer terminals, electronic pictures of a customer's whole file. This system allows faster and higher-capacity service order fulfillment by USAA. It also enriches the work, allowing service reps to make decisions on the spot without the necessity of manually checking files—and thereby keeping customers happier.

As technology advances, some services can be offered in far more sites. Today, supermarket shoppers at some locations can bank, buy stamps, and rent videos right in these stores. Coca-Cola, in blueprinting order fulfillment systems in movie theaters, identified snack food lineups as a real profit inhibitor for theater operators. Since 80 percent of a theater's profits often come from the candy counter, patrons turned off by slow-moving lines represent lost profit opportunities. Coca-Cola is experimenting with modular self-serve drink and popcorn dispensing stations to cut waiting time at the concessions. The new units have been designed to fit almost any theater's size.

In a product business, order fulfillment technology can be just as important. Hallmark, the giant in greeting cards, uses state-of-the-art warehousing and reorder systems to ensure that its 32,000 different card designs reach its 65,000 U.S. store locations in just the right quantities and at just the right time for major occasions such as Easter, Christmas, Mother's Day, and Valentine's Day.

Without such an order fulfillment system, profits would evaporate in the need to carry excess inventories or through too many out-of-stock card situations. As one executive of Hallmark pointed out, despite Hallmark's size, it makes its money "fifty cents at a time,"[11] making technology investments in order fulfillment a key management imperative.

Order Replenishment: Wal-Mart's Knockout Punch

In 1979, Wal-Mart was a small, 229-store retailer in the South, with revenues per store of a little more than $3 million. By 1989, its sales per square foot, inventory turns, and operating profits were the industry's highest. By 1992, Wal-Mart was the highest-profit and largest retailer in the world. Its 32 percent return on equity had pushed its stock price to ten times the company's book value.

What accounts for Wal-Mart's incredible success? The Boston Consulting Group, in looking at this issue in detail, concluded that Wal-Mart's knockout punch against competitors like Kmart involved a logistics system called cross-docking that allows unprecedented efficiencies in inventory replenishment. These cost savings in turn allow Wal-Mart to pursue its industry's lowest retail prices. Cross-docking involves Wal-Mart in placing full truckload orders with 4,000 vendors, receiving these goods in its nineteen distribution centers, unpacking these goods, repacking them in the configuration needed by *each* individual store, and dispatching these on its 2,000 company-owned trucks to its stores. It does all this in forty-eight hours so that, in essence, goods received move straight from the receiving docks to the shipping docks, hence the term *cross-docking*. This fast throughput system means that Wal-Mart saves 2 to 3 percent of sales by avoiding warehousing and inventory handling costs. In order to make such a system work, Wal-Mart had to invest in four strategic logistics systems: (1) a private satellite communication system to send store point-of-sale data to its 4,000 vendors; (2) a fast, company-controlled fleet of 2,000 trucks; (3) nineteen distribution centers, where it does its repacking/consolidation of orders per store; and (4) an interactive video link to allow its store managers to talk with one another and with headquarters to ensure that hot items (fast-selling goods) or "dogs" (slow movers) are identified quickly so that order replenishment can be adjusted on-the-fly.

The 2-to-3-percent cost-saving allows Wal-Mart to keep its everyday prices low. Its frequent interstore contact, which adjusts optimum orders quickly, means that it needs fewer promotions and markdowns to get rid of slow movers and excess inventories. Fewer promotions mean that sales are more predictable, and with less discounting on spot sales, Wal-Mart can afford to reward its store-level personnel with profit-sharing plans geared to in-store customer service excellence. All of founder Sam Walton's inspirational speeches to his people about excellence in customer service are premised on Wal-Mart's logistics system, which allows them to offer the best deals in town and to have just the right stock on hand to merchandise.

Order Fulfillment Service Standards

To get real continuous improvement in order fulfillment systems, management must often set tough standards for its systems and people. For instance, American Express set a standard of 100 percent accuracy within twenty-four hours for customer service personnel to respond to card member inquiries.[12]

At Deluxe Corporation, America's premier check printer, order fulfillment targets are to ship correctly next day all check orders received. Deluxe has maintained this target since 1936, almost sixty years ago, and it continues to measure its performance against this target. In 1990, its success rate was close to 95 percent of target.

These companies subscribe to the belief that order fulfillment only happens if tough goals are set, published, and measured. Order fulfillment is quite often a result of aggressive target setting, ongoing process redesign, and communications. The process is often more key to error-free fulfillment than the intellects of those operating the system. Antiquated processes defeat even the brightest, most motivated employees. Communicating ongoing results is also important. At Federal Express, when employees walk in the door each morning, they see the previous week's volume and the on-time shipping performance. In fact, in-house television provides details of yesterday's volumes and of potential problems coming up.

A Balanced Approach to Process Redesign

Whenever a company is seeking to improve its order fulfillment, it ought to look at four components: people, procedures, equipment, and policies. For example, consider a bank that wants to speed up teller service. It must look at its equipment configuration to see whether too few computers are shared by too many people, or whether this equipment breaks down often. It has to consider whether its tellers are trained and motivated to provide faster service. If not, perhaps the bank needs a training or recognition program for them. Are its procedures proper? Perhaps its bank supervisors are unrealistically assigning customer workloads, or maybe its tellers have to perform tasks—such as posting ledger entries, which is better done in nonpeak hours—that directly take away from speedy customer service. From a policy viewpoint, the bank may need to look at whether its philosophy is indeed "fast service" or whether "economical service" (from the bank's view) is being telegraphed to its people. In this latter case, it had better reorder its policy priorities, moving away from the bottom line to caring about and fixing customer service problems.

Order Follow-Up and Customer Retention

If customers are assets, clearly they should be valued for the long term. A loyal grocery store customer will spend $50,000 over a decade, a loyal customer of a car dealer $150,000 over the buyer's lifetime, and a small Federal Express account $180,000 over ten years—if account loyalty can be maintained. Proactive customer retention programs are highly efficient in the sense that they keep customer turnover low. Unhappy customers cost companies a lot of money. When they switch their business, the company loses revenue and gross margin and must spend heavily to find new customers to replace them. Unhappy customers also tell anywhere from five to eight other customers of the company's poor treatment of them, often causing a negative bandwagon effect. Of course, one of the reasons for this negative bandwagon effect is that companies have complex and cumbersome complaint procedures. They are slow to give refunds or are too quick to cite exceptions to warranty policies, when they should be concentrating on correcting the problems brought to their attention. For customers, after-sale failure costs can be severe, including anything from repair costs and transaction costs (in ordering parts or contacting the supplier) to downtime costs (if the product's downtime idles paid staff) and opportunity costs (if a product, such as an idle airliner or piece of construction equipment, could otherwise have been earning revenues).[13]

One way to boost the responsiveness and customer satisfaction results from a customer service system is to establish a routine of visiting customers on-site, using customer service representatives and documenting all the customers' unique requirements (or needs for special services). 3M maintains this practice of putting together detailed customer specification files that outline how the customer prefers to be shipped and billed, including:

- Terms of payment
- Preferred carriers to use
- Methods of shipping (pallets, truck loads)
- How pallets are to be assorted (e.g., doesn't mind mixed product assortments or wishes each pallet segregated by product line)
- Whether pallets are to be recycled
- Nature of preferred packaging (shrink-wrapped, shrouded)
- What days of the week and hours of the day are preferred delivery times
- Whether special labelling is desired (e.g., stamping the product with the customer's part number for ease of storage/access in *their* warehousing system)
- Whether the invoice is to be a consolidated billing (master invoice) or to be handled through electronic data interchange (EDI)
- Whether the buyer wishes the products to be bar-coded or not
- Whether the buyer wants special information reports on back-ordered product/delivery status, etc.

By meeting with customers, the customer service function establishes interpersonal ties, as well as documenting the customers'

specifications so that 3M can avoid errors, misshipments, or sending anything the way of the customer that isn't "right-the-first-
time."

Active customer retention programs have been used to great
advantage by airlines, hotels, rental car companies, and retailers.
These so-called frequent buyer programs usually reward customers with points for past purchases cashable for services, specials,
or merchandise. For example, Waldenbooks has a "preferred
reader" program, a project that encourages customer loyalty by offering special book discounts for members who buy regularly.

Zellers, Canada's largest discount merchandise chain, has its
"Club Z," a frequent customer membership plan in which shoppers accumulate points for catalog merchandise based on their
past purchases. A huge success, "Club Z" has six million Canadian shopper members in a population of only 25 million Canadi-
ans and is being enriched with spin-off services such as travel and
auto service club discounts.

Reader's Digest uses its data base on loyal subscribers to offer
a broad range of other products such as its classic book series,
videos, recorded music, and specialty magazines. Reader's Digest
has developed an ongoing customer relationship with its subscribers in nations around the world. Its renewal rate is 70 percent, and
its circulation is twenty-eight million. From its mailings, it has profiles of customer preferences for more than half of all American
households. Cultivating customer loyalty has paid off handsomely
for Reader's Digest: Its sales top $2.4 billion (1991), its profits are
over $213 million, and its return on equity is 28 percent. Retaining
customers has also given Reader's Digest one of the best balance
sheets in the industry—no debt, and, in December 1991, it had a
huge cash balance of $620 million on its books.[14]

Customer retention usually means taking responsibility for logistics service long after products have been sold. For example,
Toyota's Lexus tracks every car sold (and its service history) on a
national computer, so that every dealer nationwide can tap into the
entire maintenance history of any Lexus car owner from Miami to
Seattle. Why does Toyota do this? Because it wants its relationship
with customers *not* to end at the dealer's showroom door after purchase.

L. L. Bean right from its inception has offered a 100 percent guarantee *without a time limit.* If a customer is dissatisfied with an L. L. Bean product at any time, the customer can return it no matter when it was purchased or how long the item has been used or worn.

General Electric offers a prime example of a company that stands behind its products. Even though General Electric sold its small-appliance business to Black & Decker in 1984, when a possible fire hazard connected with some of its old General Electric coffeemakers surfaced, it organized one of the most proactive recall programs in history. It conducted a huge media blitz to publicize a toll-free number that consumers (owning its old coffeemakers) could call at any time, seven days a week, twenty-four hours a day. Any suspect coffeemakers were picked up by a General Electric-funded express service, and an incentive check for $10 was paid to any consumer who handed the coffeemakers to the express pick-up service. This program was well received by consumers, and General Electric brand loyalty was reinforced by a potentially troublesome situation. The machines were seven years old, beyond their six-year average life, yet General Electric was still willing to stand behind them with a no-hassle return/recall program. All consumers had their coffeemakers returned to them within one week of pickup, completely safe after a suitable General Electric inspection or overhaul.[15]

Logistics order fulfillment frequently allows a company to distinguish itself among its competitors. For instance, Spring Arbor Distributors has become America's premier distributor of Christian books, music, gifts, cards, and videos to Christian bookstores. Not only does it differentiate itself through its streamlined ordering system, but its order fulfillment includes providing retailers with complete ready-to-install children's sections (with shelves, posters, and signs) that help the retailers market Spring Arbor's products. This kind of value-added logistics service helped Spring Arbor grow from a $60-million distributor in 1986 to a $125-million distributor in fiscal 1991.

Professor Theodore Levitt of the Harvard Business School has stated that "The purpose of a business is to get and keep a customer. The sale merely consummates the courtship. How good the marriage is depends on how well the relationship is managed by the seller." While many companies pay lip service to the views aired by Levitt, not many will go to extremes to execute them, especially in logistics service. One that does is Granite Rock Company of Watsonville, California, a $90-million-per-year seller of crushed stone, concrete, and asphalt. It operates a quarry that feeds seventeen mixing plants nearby. When Granite Rock went to its customers in focus groups to ask them how its service to them could be improved, they answered, "Keep the quarry open twenty-four hours a day and help us get in to pick up loads of crushed stone as quickly as possible."

Granite Rock responded to the challenge. It invested in a state-of-the-art loading system called Granite Xpress. Truckers can drive into the quarry, check their order on the computer, stick a magnetic card into a slot, and then load their own custom order from overhead bins that operate twenty-four hours a day. This system, almost like an automated teller machine, has cut the time a trucker takes to pick up a load from thirty minutes to ten.[16]

Figure 7-5 summarizes process improvement tactics that boost logistics and customer service performance. Each in its way assures customers of fast, friendly, focused, and flexible service before, during, and after sale.

Figure 7-5. Initiatives in process improvement for logistics and customer service.

- Toll-free or fax ordering
- EDI systems—computer-to-computer orders
- Automated warehousing equipment and systems
- Bar code scanners for materials management
- Customer satisfaction measurements
- State-of-the-art complaint handling systems and guarantees
- Front-line employee empowerment/training on customer handling
- Cross-functional teams for time-compressed right-the-first-time service
- Recognition and incentives to reward top-notch service performers
- Customer information for data base management and proactive value-added service offerings
- Customer continuity (frequent buyer) programs

Notes

1. Neil Novich, "Getting the Most From Distribution," *National Productivity Review*, Vol. 10, No. 2 (Spring 1991), pp. 216–217.
2. "Cutting Out the Middleman," *Forbes* (January 6, 1992), p. 169 (with retail competitor data on p. 170).
3. Roger Calantone and Jule Gassenheimer, "Overcoming Basic Problems Between Manufacturers and Distributors," *Industrial Marketing Management Journal* (August 1991), pp. 215–221.
4. For a fuller discussion of these methods, see Allan J. Magrath, *Market Smarts—Proven Strategies to Outfox and Outflank Your Competition* (New York: John Wiley & Sons, 1988), p. 218.
5. David Evans, "The Myth of Customer Service," *Canadian Business* (March 1991), p. 36.
6. A Learning International Inc. (of Stamford, Conn.) study reported this in "Three Steps to Better Customer Service," *Personnel Journal*, Vol. 68, No. 9 (September 1991), p. 19.
7. "Profiles in Quality—Focus on Aetna Canada," in the University of Toronto's *Service Focus* newsletter (Winter 1992), p. 4 (published by the Institute of Market-Driven Quality, Toronto, Ontario).
8. W. H. Davidow and B. Uttal, "Coming: The Customer Service Decade," *Across the Board* (November 1989), p. 36.
9. Patricia Sellers, "Getting Customers to Love You," *Fortune* (March 13, 1989), p. 40.
10. Valarie Zeithaml, A. Parasuraman, and Leonard Berry, *Delivering Quality Service* (New York: The Free Press, 1990), pp. 161, 162.
11. Eva Kiess-Moser, "Customer Satisfaction," *Canadian Business Review* (Summer 1989), p. 44.
12. Robert McGough, "Pansies Are Green," *Forbes* (February 10, 1986), pp. 89–92.
13. For a complete discussion of fixed and variable costs as affected by after-sale product problems, see Miliand Lele, *The Customer Is Key* (New York: John Wiley & Sons, 1987), pp. 194–207.

14. For a corporate profile of *Reader's Digest*, see Richard Teitelbaum, "Are Times Tough? Here's an Answer," *Fortune* (December 2, 1991), pp. 101–102.
15. Barry Farber and Joyce Wycoff, "Customer Service: Evolution and Revolution," *Sales and Marketing Management* (May 1991), pp. 46, 47.
16. John Case, "The Change Masters," *Inc.* magazine (March 1991), p. 61.

8

The Planning System

Strategic thinking describes what a company does in becoming smart, targeted, and nimble enough to prosper in an era of constant change.

Ronald Henkoff
Associate Editor, Fortune

Planning systems balance a company's ambitions against the reality of business conditions. Improving the quality of planning involves a company in looking for improved yield in the three key areas of planning: spotting/sizing up opportunities; formulating possible strategies and then selecting the one that best matches the spotted opportunity with the company's skill sets and capacities; and executing the plan fast but in a way that allows for refinements along the way and avoids betting the company on a specific strategy. Sometimes opportunity-spotting will uncover markets where a company must stretch its skills or resources in order to succeed. Where this is the case, the planning system needs to consider how to creatively attack the opportunity, since it lies somewhat outside the resources or skills the company currently possesses.

Opportunity size-ups require good market research and a feel for untapped customer needs. Apple Computer unlocked previously untapped home computing needs when it debuted its easy-to-use Macintosh to the world of computing. In addition, good planning involves the ability to spot opportunities that a rival may not have seen.

For instance, The Gap, one of America's most successful niche retailers (which does over $2 billion a year in sales and makes $180 million-plus in profit while doing it!), is constantly trying to figure out what people want to wear in reasonably priced casual clothing so that it can offer clothes that change but that don't go out of style after only one season. The Gap tunes in on its customers' needs by offering sizing that fits changing body shapes. Its jeans come in four basic cuts for women and three for men. It's tuned in especially to the changing needs of the baby boomer generation. And as boomers' life-styles and values have shifted to their families, The Gap has been there with 213 Gap Kids stores, selling smaller versions of Gap T-shirts, jeans, and sweaters.[1]

The Charles Schwab Corporation is a fine example of a company that is good at sizing up competitive openings. Schwab is the largest discount stockbroker in the United States, and it got that way by realizing it needed to offer more service than did its even lower-priced rivals (such as Quick & Reilly, which charge $49 per 100 shares traded), but less service than full-service brokers such as Merrill Lynch at $85 per 100 shares traded. At $55 Schwab falls between bare-bones, Woolworth-type service but below Nordstrom-type, hand-holding, full-broker service. The huge middle of the market is what it targeted. And it executed its strategy with seven-days-a-week, twenty-four-hours-a-day service availability. In fact, owners of personal computers can trade electronically by modem with Schwab, as can investors who can enter trades on touch-tone telephones. In an average day, more than 26 percent of Schwab's trades are done using these two customer-friendly "no fuss" methods.

Successful companies such as The Gap and Charles Schwab recognize that to stay ahead they must be adaptive, learning organizations, so they gear their planning systems to opportunity-spotting with an eye on both customers and competitors.

Spotting Bad Plans and Being Responsive

A planning system with integrity ought also to be able to spot where a company is spinning its wheels and making wasteful resource decisions in chasing markets in which it doesn't belong. So it's essential that plans be reviewed with realistic sets of milestones, so the company can know when to jettison a bad plan. For instance, Anheuser-Busch bought majority interest in Exploration Cruise Lines in 1985, as part of its Busch entertainment unit (which owns Busch Gardens in Tampa, Cypress Gardens, and Sea World), but its planning system did not anticipate the downturn in cruise-line profits as the cruise industry consolidated.[2] Busch was smart enough in its planning review process, however, to pull the plug on the cruise line in 1987 as its earlier rosy hopes were shattered by operating realities. When Bausch and Lomb's planning system showed that it couldn't meet its margin goals with two of its large operations, prescription eyeglasses and industrial instruments, it divested itself of these to concentrate on better opportunities with its Ray-Ban sunglasses line.

So a company's planning system must be responsive enough to blaze new trails but also savvy enough to know when mid-course corrections to plans are called for.

Finding an Operating Focus

When a company is chasing market or competitor openings, its plans need to spell out explicitly how the company's resources should be channeled to seize the opening. So at Lens Crafters, plans focus on operating at top speed with systems that provide rapid turnaround on customer eyeglass orders. First Wachovia Bank and Trust of North Carolina emphasizes relationship banking in its plans, so its operating focus is on excellent data base management of repeat-customer needs. H&R Block's plans would emphasize low cost, so its operating focus and systems are geared to volume. Frito-Lay's plans would emphasize market coverage and snack food share, so its operating focus would be on logistics and new snack brands. Braun's plans would emphasize bringing uniqueness to established small-appliance markets, so its operating focus is on superior design of its shavers, coffeemakers, and food processors.

Figure 8-1 models the planning system components and the key issues inherent in ensuring that each component's yield is as high as possible.

Figure 8-1. Planning system components and yield issues.

Opportunity Size-Ups (market or competitive openings)

Are enough opportunities being identified and scoped by the planning system for optimum growth?

Too few   =   Low yield
Too many   =   Lack of focus, dispersed resources, and low yield per
                    opportunity

Strategy Selection

Does the plan spell out strategy alternatives, the risks inherent in each, the potential payoffs, and the operating priority that must be emphasized for such payoffs?

Strategy Execution/Refinement Review

Does the planning review system help point up wasteful or faulty plans that require responsive turnarounds or divestiture?

The Value of Clear Goals

When a company's goals are very clear and explicit, planning becomes much more productive. For instance, it was Rubbermaid's goal in the 1980s to double sales, profits, and earnings per share every five years. It wanted to be the low-cost producer in its markets *and* the brand recognition/quality leader. So its planning system had to be able to produce lots of opportunity-spotting, since rapid-growth aspirations dictated this. And it had to have a planning system that emphasized multiple strategies, because any single strategy, such as new products alone, acquisitions alone, or overseas expansion alone, would likely have been insufficient to meet its growth goals. In fact, its then-chairman, Stanley Gault, pushed the planning system to seek multiple market inputs on opportunities (lots of focus groups with customers, formal market studies, and prescribed time in the field in stores by Rubbermaid personnel) and to make use of eight separate strategies: four for incremental growth and four for what Gault called "leap growth."

Figure 8-2 outlines Rubbermaid's strategy selection menu from its planning system.

Meshing Plans With the Company's Risk Comfort

All strategy selection involves assessing risks, and, in Rubbermaid's case, its appetite for risk was high. But not all companies are so comfortable with risks. For example, when it comes to strategy selection, many companies prefer not to diversify but rather to seek more growth in their current market. They aren't comfortable with new market risks. Reader's Digest has grown its sales to over $2.4 billion by selling recorded music, books, videos, and specialty magazines to the existing customer base for its *Reader's Digest* magazine. It has done this so successfully that only 28 percent of its total sales and 31 percent of its profits in 1992 came from its *Reader's Digest* subscriptions around the world. The planning system sought higher yield by mining existing customer data bases rather than by going into new businesses.

Between 1980 and 1988, Tyson Farms increased sales of its

Figure 8-2. Rubbermaid's strategy selections.

For: *Incremental Growth*

1. Sell more of existing products via better quality, lower costs, better service.
2. Upscale products with new colors.
3. Extend product lines by way of new sizes and spinoffs.
4. Expand geographically in Europe.

For: *"Leap Growth"*

1. Develop new products (with a 30 percent new products target).
2. Enter new markets (every 18 to 24 months).
3. Acquire new companies.
4. Diversify through joint ventures with outside partners.

Source: Adapted from a speech by Stanley Gault, CEO of Rubbermaid, *Conference Board of Canada*, Toronto, Ontario, Canada, 15th Annual Marketing Conference, Hilton International, March 29, 1990.

chicken products by over a billion dollars. What masterstroke of strategy selection did it use? None at all; Tyson simply decided to begin offering many more varieties of chicken, from chicken parts, to gourmet dinners, to microwaveable chicken and precooked varieties. More than sixty varieties of chicken were offered. Its planning system spotted the fact that more niches for its existing product were there in the market just waiting to be tapped.[3] Bell of Pennsylvania grew its business by bundling four special services (call waiting, call forwarding, three-way calling, and speed calling) at an attractive packaged price. Its market research showed untapped potential, so it selected a very low-risk but (as it turned out) high payoff strategy.

Sifting for Niches

Planning systems have to be responsive enough to constantly sift for these niche-broadening possibilities. Sony is a fine example of a company whose trend-spotting often leads others. Between 1979 and 1989, its Walkman has been continually decked out with improvements to keep its appeal strong. Figure 8-3 lists eleven product improvements added to the basic Walkman since 1979. (These are quite apart from the new *models* launched, such as Sony's Sports Walkman.)

When planning systems monitor markets for opportunities, a

Figure 8-3. Improvements made to Sony's Walkman, 1979–1989.

1. Auto reverse added
2. Bass-treble controls added
3. Special, smaller headphones added
4. Basic unit downsized
5. Units made shock-resistant
6. Units made water-resistant
7. Electronic tuning added
8. Made smaller again
9. Units made rechargeable
10. Dolby sound added
11. Alarm clock feature added

company needs to use its judgment in a way that goes beyond merely tuning in on consumer opinion. For instance, Levi Strauss did research in the 1980s that showed that consumers' *expressed* concerns about fitness were very high, and, if they were to be believed, consumers would all be getting in shape and need the tightest, form-fittingest jeans around. But Levi Strauss planners, looking beyond what people were saying to what they were actually doing, saw a lot more people walking than jogging or running. So they launched Dockers brand jeans, whose main selling feature is a roomier waist. Because of their astute judgment, sales of Dockers have climbed to over $800 million worldwide, as customers' real need for roomier jeans outweighed their good intentions about upgrading their personal fitness.

Going Beyond the Superficial

Two of the biggest mistakes a new opportunity size-up can make are superficially overestimating new opportunity potential and overlooking the large potential still left in the company's core products.

Federal Express, aware that the single-market European Economic Community was looming in 1992, was guilty of rushing into Europe to build a delivery service in anticipation of the European market becoming as large as the American market. This was a pie-in-the-sky assessment since daily intra-European traffic in express packages never exceeded 150,000, versus three million packages a day crossing state lines in the United States. The result has been a fiasco for Federal, and it has had to substantially roll back its plans for Europe; in fact, Federal is subcontracting to locals much of the market opportunity. Federal Express was guilty of placing more credence in the hype about the EC than in the facts of current market demand, and then of not probing more deeply to see what would fundamentally alter these.[4]

The major athletic sock manufacturers in America are guilty of overlooking the potential left in their core products, and as a result they have lost the market to a newcomer, Thor-Lo. Three giant mills—Wigwam, Fox River, and Burlington—dominated the marketing and sale of white (or striped) cotton athletic socks. But they treated the business as a commodity in a mature industry, and they stopped looking for new market niches. In this regard, their planning systems failed them.

Along came an upstart company, Thor-Lo Inc., which added special padding for specific sports, eighteen in all, including "sports-specific" socks for tennis, aerobics, basketball, golf, cycling, and hiking. Each sports-specific design puts the socks' padding where the foot takes the most pounding, and sports enthusiasts, who for years have wanted a more comfortable sock, have demonstrated their approval to the tune of $30 million in sales for Thor-Lo.

Sometimes the big players in a market overlook opportunities right in front of their noses because they are too close to them. For instance, Coca-Cola practically invented vending as a distribution channel for soft drinks. Yet its very own Minute Maid division overlooked the vending of single-serving juices and gave the market up to Verifine Products, Ocean Spray, Mott's, and Welch's, all much smaller competitors than Minute Maid in mainstream supermarket distribution.

Benckiser Consumer Products, which markets Electrasol automatic dishwasher detergent (9 percent market share), has been the most innovative of competitors in this business, despite being dwarfed by Procter & Gamble's Cascade (50 percent market share) and Lever Brothers' Sunlight (20 percent market share). Benckiser recently sensed a market need for superconcentrated automatic dishwasher detergent to rid consumers' concerns about waste and the environment. This segment had been overlooked by the giants in the business.

Sound Competitor Mapping

A sound planning system yields a solid understanding and map of competitors' positions in the different parts of the market. For instance, in the computer industry, hundreds of companies compete, each possessing different strengths and resources. Yet it is possible, with an excellent planning system, to categorize these companies into five groups on the basis of how they compete.

1. *Broad-range competitors* compete across multiple products, including mainframes, midrange computers, personal computers, peripherals, software, and services. IBM is the best example of this kind of company.

2. *Geographically restricted competitors* limit their sales efforts to specific regions or customers. ICL in the United Kingdom is in this group.

3. *Niche competitors* compete in only one product segment, such as personal computers, laptops, workstations, or printers/peripherals. Companies such as Dell, Toshiba, Silicon Graphics, and Sun Microsystems are in this category.

4. *Application or specific-solution providers* base their competitive edge on in-depth skills in software or related services. Companies such as Lotus and Microsoft are in this focused area.

5. *Integrated-solution providers* bring wide-spectrum technologies and products to customers who need complex systems solutions. Electronic Data Systems (EDS) and Anderson Consulting are such competitors.

From this sort of mapping, a company such as IBM can determine how much of the market and its total profitability is shifting to software and systems integration services (categories 4 and 5 above) from hardware platforms, be they mainframes, personal computers, or peripherals. Within categories, it can also plot its vulnerabilities and strengths. For instance, in certain niches IBM is far weaker than it is overall in that it has only a 20 percent share of the $53-billion storage products market and a 10 percent share of the $30-billion printer market.[5]

This sort of competitor mapping can also help a company spot opportunities. IBM, for example, has spotted an opportunity inside category 4 for software useful to service businesses, which it believes will grow as service industries expand their GNP share. IBM sees a gap here between what is offered by Lotus, Intergraph, and others and what customers may need, so it is investing to produce such software.

Figure 8-4 diagrams this competitor mapping. As technologies blur, clearly defined segments such as mainframes, minis, and personal computers also blur because networked personal

Figure 8-4. A competitor map of the computer industry.

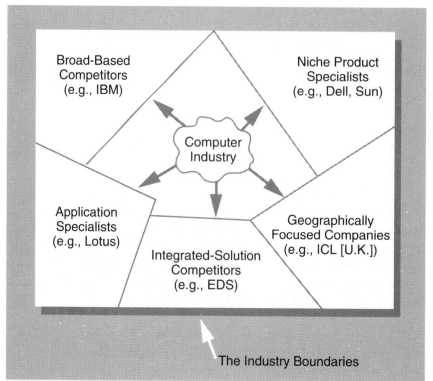

computers may be able to offer a customer just as much computing power as a mainframe. Planning systems that map competitive categories well can also act as guides to defining the skills needed to compete in each part of the map. For example, integrated-solution companies need exterior consulting skills and third-party sourcing, whereas specific-application companies need deep software and service expertise as it relates to very narrow market needs. Niche hardware firms such as Hewlett-Packard often compete on the basis of speed, flexibility, technological leadership, and competitive costs, while broad-range competitors such as IBM emphasize account control, knowledge, and sales-marketing support conferred by their scale or size.

If an IBM wants a bigger stake in peripherals (category 3) or software-specific solutions (category 4), it must alter its skill set to be more flexible and fast in "hot" niche products or deepen its expertise in software development. These may be skills that do not comprise core capabilities of IBM, and so must be acquired in order to shift category emphasis. This becomes a great challenge to a broad-based competitor such as IBM because thinning margins in personal computers and slower overall growth in mainframes pinch its financial resources just at a time when it needs to move into newer, faster-growing market categories.

A planning system that exposes for review a competitor's Achilles' heel often yields dramatic results.

In 1990, Ford Motor caught Chrysler's Jeep division napping by launching an alternative to Jeep in its Ford Explorer, which combined three elements Jeep lacked. The Explorer featured improved safety equipment such as rear shoulder belts, was easier to switch into four-wheel drive (by pushing a button as opposed to shifting an awkward lever on the Jeep), and offered style (leather interiors) at $4,500 below Jeep's price. Explorer's sales pushed Ford from an 18 percent to a 25 percent share in off-road vehicles, as Jeep's share fell from 24 percent to 20 percent.[6]

Customer Perception Mapping

Just as competitors can be mapped, so too can customers' perceptions of products. A planning system ought to map perceptions of products along the attributes customers view as key. For example, in over-the-counter pain relievers, customer-mapped perceptions (in Canada) showed that three product attributes (pricing, pain-relieving effectiveness, and gentleness on the stomach) were primary, while three other attributes (ease in swallowing, safe for children, long-lasting) were perceived as also important but secondary. A perceptual map of where the leading products fit could be developed based on market research.

Figure 8-5 shows a hypothetical perceptual product map for seven pain relievers. By mapping product perceptions, a brand's marketer can look for brand repositioning possibilities. For instance, Bayer might want to try and reposition its brand so that it is perceived as stronger in effectiveness, while Anacin's brand manager might want to reposition its pain reliever as longer-lasting

Figure 8-5. A perceptual product map for pain relievers (using hypothetical data).

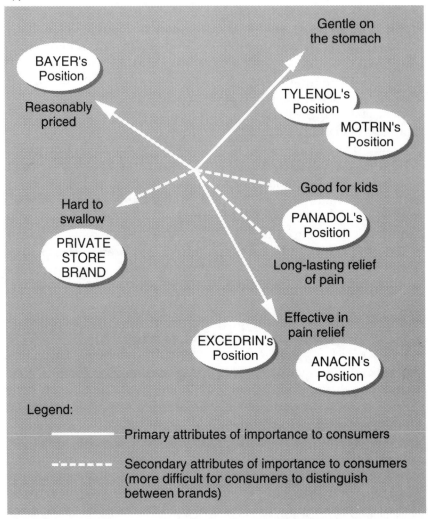

Adapted from Marshall Rice, Associate Professor, Faculty of Administrative Studies, York University, Toronto, Canada, "A User's Guide to Product/Perceptual Mapping," *Imprints,* the newsletter of the Professional Market Research Society of Canada (April 1992), p. 17.

so as to differentiate it more clearly from Excedrin and avoid too much brand switching among its target consumers. Panadol (in the center of the map), with no real distinguishing position, would have to consider developing a brand personality that moves it out of the pack on an attribute of more buying importance to consumers.

Sometimes the introduction of a new product can alter the entire perceptual product map. Procter & Gamble is trying to do this with its new Citrus Hill Orange Juice with calcium. By fortifying its juice with calcium, the company hopes to (1) convince families that orange juice can build bones just as milk can and (2) alter the entire perception of orange juice as simply a good-tasting source of vitamin C.

Strategy Selection

While the front end of the planning system must do a good job identifying opportunities in the market, the system must also spell out strategy options to capitalize on these opportunities. Some systems, such as Rubbermaid's, identify multiple strategies for successful growth, and this is the case with many large companies. The problem of growing a large base of sales to an even bigger base without many different strategies is major. A single type of strategy simply does not provide enough growth momentum. For instance, Nestlé, at $36 billion-plus in annual sales, must use multiple strategy levers to grow. It uses acquisitions, joint ventures, new products, and market penetration simultaneously. In acquisitions, it bought up the United States' Carnation, Britain's Rowntree, and Italy's Buitoni-Perugina (pasta) to expand its product mix. It has joint ventures with General Mills (to distribute General Mills cereals in Europe) and with Coca-Cola (to have Coke distribute its Nestlé iced teas). It has launched new products such as Lean Cuisine frozen foods as well as sought deeper market penetration in Asia (especially in China and Myanmar, formerly Burma).

In smaller companies, planning yield is usually accomplished by narrowing strategy selections so as to concentrate resources and boost the organization's skill set to competitive levels. For example, BE Avionics is a small California maker of video systems and seat controls for aircraft seats. (It had $68 million in sales in 1991.) Its competitors are Sony and Matsushita, giants that are diversified in all sorts of electronic products. So BE Avionics has kept its strategy selection very narrow by choosing to acquire other small companies making products that sell to its same base, aircraft customers. It recently acquired companies that make high-tech aircraft kitchen hardware and another one that refurbishes aircraft seats. By concentrating on synergistic acquisitions, BE Avionics can have its sales engineers, who call on the major airlines, sell a broader product offering. Small companies usually learn rapidly that focus is the only way to get effective yield from their planning. Trying to be too flexible—ready for too many different opportunities and executing too many varied strategies—often means that the company never masters anything well, which puts it in the position of not being good at anything.

Centering the Planning System Close to the Market

Strategy selections need to be made by the business teams closest to the action in the trenches. In Japan this is often termed *Genba*, which means that the people who make the decisions must actually be on the scene of events to know them firsthand. Making strategy selections in the cloistered precincts of headquarters offices is usually a sure-fire way to screw up. Nissan during the 1980s did the worst job of strategy selection in the American market of all Japanese auto builders. It failed to practice *Genba*. At a time when most Japanese car makers' shares increased, Nissan U.S.A.'s fell from 5.5 percent in 1980 to 4.7 percent in 1991. (During the same period, Japan's overall share rose from 17.7 percent to 28.5 percent.) Why did this occur? Nissan chose its strategies back in Tokyo instead of letting its Nissan U.S.A. company fashion a made-in-America strategy. Tokyo decided it could continue to try and sell small sporty cars, and ignored the family sedan and mini-van segments. Honda and Toyota stole this market opportunity with Accord and Camry. Nissan Tokyo spent its dealer development funds on its Japanese dealers, ignoring its U.S. dealers, who needed support, direction, and network pruning to weed out the very poorest ones (and help those remaining to become stronger). In 1990, whereas 70 percent-plus of Toyota's and Honda's U.S. dealers were happy with their dealer franchises, only 20 percent of Nissan's were happy. The parent company should have let its U.S. planners drive the planning rather than allow Tokyo to second-guess them.[7]

Contrast Nissan's approach with that of Johnson & Johnson, whose 166 different business units do their own autonomous planning. Johnson & Johnson grew by 50 percent between 1987 and 1991, its new products are flourishing under this autonomous planning, and it has brand leadership not only in its core units (such as health care) but in newer units such as its disposable contact lens business. Units close to customers can respond quickly to fluid opportunities, and they tend to formulate strategy with their fingertips by virtue of their product, distribution, and pricing decisions.

Reacting to Serendipitous Opportunities

Decentralizing planning to boost yield has another benefit beyond being more in touch with customer or competitor pressures. When a market takes off, quite unexpectedly, a decentralized group doing the planning and strategy selection can react much more rapidly. Johnson & Johnson's smaller entrepreneurial units are running all out in two businesses in which demand is far outstripping predictions—in sales of disposable contact lenses, which grew 50 percent per year in 1991, and sales of endoscopic surgical instruments (for noninvasive surgery), which are growing in the 100-percent-per-year range.

Fuji U.S.A. has had to run very fast with its strategies to capture the surprisingly strong demand for single-use cameras. These cameras sold ten million units per year in the United States after only four years of being on the market. Fuji's planning systems are flexible enough to accommodate such fast-breaking products, for which demand is doubling every two years.

Rubbermaid uses small teams centered around product lines to come up with their own plans and strategies, and these teams often involve all cross-functional disciplines, including research and distribution, engineering, manufacturing, sales, marketing, finance, and information systems personnel. Rubbermaid then ties financial rewards to reviews of team performance against the plan as a way of reinforcing discipline and providing visible recognition for these autonomous units.

Conducting Business Reviews

At some point, management must review plans and either pronounce them sound on the basis of their yield and good sense or suggest that they be altered. High-yield planning systems are subject to this review/revise activity so as to minimize paperwork, formality, and destructive criticism of the plan owners. The process should be kept short, and it ought to maximize discussion, consensus building, and informality. Too much formality inhibits discussion and debate, the very thing most often needed when reviews are held. Too many forms or excessive paperwork in preparing for reviews chews up management time better devoted to implementing, fixing, and improving plans and execution. In a world where nonlinear events often shape opportunities, crafting the perfect one-time plan and spending hours defending it are wasteful of energy, enthusiasm, and talent.

Southern California Edison, an electric utility in California, used to plan for the long range in great detail until it took a look at past strategic plans and found that every plan had been rendered obsolete by unforecasted events such as OPEC price fixing, the Chernobyl disaster, and sulfur emission restrictions. It is far better to craft succinct plans, with tight action priorities spelled out and clear measurement targets set down, and then spend the time to gain management buy-in or to revise the plan on a just-in-time basis.

Nestlé used to review its businesses endlessly at multiple levels in headquarters, even requiring its operating units to prepare twenty-five-page monthly reports of how they were doing against the plan's targets. Today, it has streamlined all this, and units report back, on only one page, the key indicators of their performance versus the plan. Senior management at Nestlé now uses most of its planning review time to discuss basic strategy rather than to review all the details of its various operations. This has helped boost yield from its planning system in two ways: Operating units have more authority to move on planned marketing opportunities faster, with fewer approvals, and senior management has been able to gain a better consensus (because of its emphasis on strategy versus business unit details) about sharing marketing strategies *across* business units.[8]

Lean Cuisine, for example, was transplanted from the United States to Europe because plan discussions showed that British and other overseas consumers would also react well to the product line,

Figure 8-6. A summary of planning system yield: process improvements.

Opportunity Size-Ups	Key Process: Sensing the Environment
	o Map competitors.
	o Map product perceptions of customers.
	o Set operating focus.
	o Identify poor fits and where size-ups suggest divestiture.
Strategy Selection	Key Process: Focus and Risk Assessment
	o Identify strategy array (multiple or single vectors).
	o Center planning in business units close to market.
	o Use planning teams that are multifunctional in scope.
	o Gear rewards to plan results.
	o Build in flexibility in case different scenarios develop.
Strategy Execution/ Review/Revision	Key Processes: Simplification and Dialogue
	o Minimize forms, paperwork.
	o Maximize discussion, informality.
	o Minimize length and number of reviews per year.
	o Build consensus about necessary strategic shifts.

originally marketed only in America. At Southern California Edison, plans represent scenario responses to possible events in which each scenario could trigger different power generation strategies, from repowering oil and gas power generating plants to buying extra power from other vendors. A quality mind-set applied to the review process of business plans looks for cycle time improvements by eliminating wasted paperwork and management time (in too many reviews or overly long ones). It also looks for flexibility should a different future materialize.

Figure 8-6 summarizes the process improvement priorities for improved planning system yield. In all three phases of planning — opportunity size-up, strategy selection, and plan review/revision — continuous improvements can often be made that keep this system responsive, focused, and productive.

Notes

1. Susan Caminiti, "The Gap: Reading the Customer Right," *Fortune* (December 2, 1991), p. 106.
2. Seth Lubove, "Unfinished Business," *Forbes* (December 10, 1990), p. 172.
3. Orbert E. Linneman and John L. Stanton, Jr., "Mining for Niches," *Business Horizons* (May-June 1992), p. 47.
4. "Federal Express Passes the Parcel," *The Economist* (March 21, 1992), p. 73.
5. "Scenting Extinction," *The Economist* (December 14, 1991), pp. 69–70.
6. James Treece and Mark Landler, "Beep, Beep! There Goes Ford's Explorer," *Business Week* (January 28, 1991), pp. 60–61.
7. K. Miller, L. Armstrong, and J. Treece, "Will Nissan Get It Right This Time?" *Business Week* (April 20, 1992), pp. 82–87.
8. Jay Palmer, "The Chocolate Juggernaut," *Barron's* (July 8, 1991), p. 13.

Epilogue: Achieving Zero-Defect Marketing

Substantial gains (in business results) come from gutsy unreasonable ideas, not play-it-safe tinkering with the status quo.

Charles R. Day, Jr.
Editor-in-Chief, Industry Week

Process redesign has significantly improved the competitiveness of U.S. factories. From 1985 to 1992, labor costs per unit of output fell 42 percent against benchmarked unit labor costs of the United States' major trading partners, and the number of U.S. employees per million dollars of manufacturing gross domestic product (GDP) has been cut almost in half since 1975. All of the attention to manufacturing process automation, simplification and focusing, waste reduction, retraining, and the tools of total quality management is paying off behind the factory gate and warehouse door. Unfortunately, the front-end functions in most companies have not improved their processes or white-collar productivity, and this includes marketing's part of the equation. White-collar productivity is not much better than it was in 1975, and much of this lack of progress can be attributed to corporations' failing to apply total quality management principles to selling, advertising, product line management, and the many other systems that comprise value-added activities beyond the manufacturing/warehousing chain. Self-managed, empowered teams and employee involvement programs in redesigning the tasks of marketing are visibly lacking in too many companies. As a result, many marketing systems are still too complex, waste-ridden, and unresponsive to customers or fleet-

155

ing market opportunities. Decision making is often slow and bureaucratic, yields from marketing systems weak or uneven (such as new product or ad campaign successes), and many processes performed as they were years ago, when competition was less intense, prices more bullish, and margins fatter.

As a result, while the unit costs of marketing are up, overall efficiency has not significantly improved. Two glaring cases in point are IBM and General Motors, each of which has lost market share and suffered customer defections in key segments of its business while costs have soared and profits plummeted. Only a concerted effort to overhaul the processes of front-end marketing will boost efficiency and U.S. competitiveness. Nowadays, customers and stockholders are quick to desert or punish companies that fall out of touch with the market.

Boston University found, in a survey of white-collar cost competitiveness, that the United States lags behind Western Europe's efficiency by 20 percent and behind Japan's by 25 percent as of 1992. So major process redesign must begin on front-end marketing activities if U.S. industry is to remain competitive in the future. It's simply not good enough to continue developing products, pricing them, positioning them, distributing them, advertising them, and selling them the way these things have always been done in the past. Zero-Defect Marketing must be the goal.

Teams and More Teams

Turning marketers from being program thinkers and doers into process-oriented diagnosticians and redesigners calls for some big changes. Marketers must be able to understand and flowchart their key processes, often with the help of others, in order to put together cross-functional teams to fix these processes. For instance, boosting yield from a product innovation system means commercializing new technology faster. Clearly, what is needed to do this is a team comprised not only of marketing but also of logistics, engineering, research and development, and manufacturing personnel. Varied skills have to be integrated in such a way that the team can come up with inventive breakthroughs. The ingenuity of all group participants will need to be tapped to progress. For instance, a new automobile model in 1992 costs a billion dollars to develop and launch. To do so successfully requires the teamwork coordination of manufacturing, parts, advertising, and distribution. If any part of the process is flubbed, millions of dollars can be wasted, dealers and customers may be angered, and sales momentum lost.

In many core marketing processes, marketing must learn to share leadership if effective teamwork is to occur. The lead in any process redesign will shift often among team members whose different kinds of knowledge may confer team leadership on them at a particular point in time, as such knowledge is demanded by the specifics of the situation. Learning to share process redesign ideas is a must for marketers. Marketers must therefore learn the essentials of being good team players. This means teaming with the sales force and sales managers with respect to selling systems, with dealers concerning channel systems, with ad agencies on persuasion systems, with the warehouse on logistics systems, and so on for all of marketing's key processes.

Proactive Process Improvements

Marketing must also learn to be proactive, to seek continuous improvement without being pushed into it by poor operating results. If poor results are already turning up, a process fix is probably too late.

Consider Frito-Lay, which is altering its snack food brands Lay's and Ruffles potato chips, the two largest-selling brands in America, without reacting out of pressure. It has decided to alter the taste and texture by using a different cooking oil (cottonseed oil versus soybean oil) and a new frying technology. The new chips have more potato flavor and crispness. In neither process change case did Frito-Lay have to improve its product because of slumping market share, waning consumer loyalty, or buyer complaints. Frito-Lay was simply being proactive with the product reformulation to stay ahead of tough competition such as Anheuser-Busch, which markets Eagle brand snack foods.[1]

Aiming Process Improvements at the
Right Target—the Customer

Marketers intent on process breakthroughs must constantly re-check innovative changes with customers to make sure the customer believes that such changes are worthwhile. Allen-Bradley, a $1.4-billion Milwaukee-based manufacturer of industrial automation equipment, spent millions in the 1980s on a comprehensive quality program to continuously improve its marketing and other processes. It discovered that only meager financial gains were being reaped from such efforts, so it decided to find out why. It asked its customers for their perceptions only to discover that they didn't see the value in a lot of Allen-Bradley's changes or didn't even notice the improvements. Today, Allen-Bradley routinely measures customer expectations as it adjusts its processes instead of assuming that its customers will take notice of its continuous improvement endeavors.[2]

Johnson Controls, which makes climate control systems for office buildings, believed that customers' number one criterion in purchasing its controls was the up-front purchase price of its systems. After a two-year immersion in customer visits, Johnson's chief engineer, Hugh Hudson, discovered that customers were more concerned with the system's total cost, including installation *and* maintenance, than with the initial price/value trade-off. Johnson's systems were often hard and expensive to fix; to do so, a company had to shut down the heat or air conditioning in the entire building and also disconnect a lot of wires, thus subjecting some of its employees to the danger of electrocution. Hudson and a design team, acting to design a new system (called Metasys), created a product in which plastic modules could be easily replaced without tools or an entire system shutdown. By being focused on customer needs, Johnson Control's product innovation system improvement yielded great results. In its first year of sales alone, Johnson's product brought in $500 million in revenues.[3]

As the Johnson Controls example illustrates, getting on the same wavelength as customers about their cost concerns can be complex. Customers incur different kinds of costs related to products. These include acquisition costs of obtaining products, possession costs in storing them prior to use, training costs in learning about them, repair costs in keeping them in working order, and eventually replacement costs, as the purchase cycle begins anew.

Concentrating on Major Process Improvements

Marketing needs to focus on exponential as opposed to incremental change in its systems or subsystems. This frequently requires marketers to look outside the boundaries of current practice in the search for newer solutions. In a sense, marketers must shift the paradigm that governs the thinking and behavior surrounding how the system is routinely dealt with by itself and its rivals.

A good example of this was Honda's approach to its channel system for the sale of its motorcycles. Typically, motorcycle manufacturers sold motorcycles through local dealers who had great enthusiasm for cycling as a hobby but were only secondarily concerned with building their dealerships into strong businesses. These dealers were not particularly enamored of the marketing, management, or financial aspects involved in building a more professional dealership. Honda decided to take a different approach to its channel system. It wanted to help its dealers become successful businesspeople. It provided extensive operating manuals and procedures for selling, advertising, floor stock merchandising, and service/parts management. It gave training to its dealers and their staffs in these disciplines and supported each dealership with computerized information software and systems. The better prepared, better managed, and better financed Honda dealerships succeeded in besting the part-time dealers whose hobby interest took precedence over their operations skills. As a result, Honda took market share and outgrew its rivals with a far superior channel system. Honda's dealerships had the skills to serve new emerging "middle class" motorcyclists, instead of just the traditional avid leather-jacketed crowd. This paradigm shifting by Honda changed the basis for competing in the industry and represented a revolutionary approach versus an incremental approach to the improvement of a key marketing process-dealer management.[4]

In looking for process improvements, managements often try to limit their risk exposure by being somewhat conservative in process redesign. For instance, a company will introduce telesales in a very staged way until it has completely proved itself. Or the company will alter its merchandising price plans in only marginal ways so as not to upset its dealers—even when the evidence suggests that end customers would welcome more radical changes. Ford is taking this approach with its "one price" policy for Escorts, which has won higher acceptance among car buyers than among Ford dealers.

The problem with this approach is that such timidity also limits the company's gains from process redesign. If a company shows boldness toward process redesign in marketing, its rate of improvement versus competitors will be greater, and eventually it will surpass its rivals. It took the Japanese thirty years to catch up in manufacturing process breakthroughs such as shorter cycle times, but today they excel. Moreover, they are moving on to emphasize new process priorities in the factory such as flexible production lines, which will enable them to customize products more easily. This same mind-set is worth emulating in marketing process redesign. For instance, when Armstrong World Industries decided to redesign its customer credit handling, it sought major gains by way of automation and procedural streamlining. As a result, its customer service on damaged goods returned for credit moved from a 100-day average settlement time to two days on average.[5]

Root Cause Diagnosis of System Malfunctions

As marketers become more attuned to a process orientation, they will learn to be more astute in diagnosing the root causes of system malfunctions in marketing. As an example, Hewlett-Packard decided to analyze its accounts receivable to determine why its customers were paying so slowly. They believed that slowness in payment might be caused by uncompetitive discount terms being offered for timely payments. Instead, Hewlett-Packard discovered that its receivables problem was a direct result of poor paperwork on its own part relating to product shipments. High error rates in shipping documentation by Hewlett-Packard meant that customers were often unsure as to where or when their shipments would arrive; often they didn't know exactly what had been shipped at any point in time. Customers were signaling their displeasure by not paying on time, which showed up in accounts receivable piling up. In-depth root cause analysis greatly assists marketers in discovering what aspect of any key marketing system is really causing customer problems.[6]

The Integrated Nature of Marketing Systems

Much of this book details the different systems and processes of marketing. It then prescribes the key process variables that ought to drive continuous improvement in each system, such as waste minimization in ad media spending, higher yields in new product innovation systems, greater capacity in channel systems, higher efficiency in selling systems, and so on. But systems do not exist in isolation from one another. Without good advertising, it is tougher to get distribution channel support. Without excellent selling or incentivizing systems, product innovation opportunities will be squandered. Without a sound logistics system, channel systems will fail because of inconsistent or unreliable order processing and deliveries.

So a marketer intent on process improvements in marketing systems ought to understand the interconnectedness of its multiple systems. In this way, process improvements can be leveraged in total. For example, Goodyear Tire & Rubber is working on concurrent process improvements for (1) new products (safer rain tires); (2) new advertising/branding; and (3) new marketing channel partnerships, such as with Sears Roebuck. These three systems work symbiotically. That is, good new products with differentiation make advertising's potency greater. In addition, Goodyear's yield from gaining new distribution (via selling its tires in Sears stores) is much higher if new-to-the-world products comprise part of the new channel's mix.

Another example that demonstrates the synergy between marketing systems involves Phillips-VanHeusen's dress shirt division. VanHeusen's market share has climbed to the industry's leading position, surpassing Arrow's because at the same time that it has boosted advertising from $2.5 million in 1991 to $10 million in 1993, it has dramatically expanded its distribution channels. Its

Figure E-1. Key concepts surrounding continuous improvement worth noting by marketers.

1. Learn to work smoothly with teams.
2. Be proactive. Don't wait till you're pressured into change.
3. Aim process improvements at customers.
4. Work for exponential gains from process redesign.
5. Look for root causes when diagnosing marketing system bottlenecks.
6. Recognize the integrated nature of all marketing systems.

Figure E-2. What is process improvement in marketing?

It Is NOT	*It IS*
A new marketing program	A new way of managing marketing
Looking for overnight miracles in marketing practice	Continuous improvements over the long haul in marketing practice and systems
Fire fighting, crisis management, or reacting to customers	A structured, team-driven, disciplined approach to higher customer satisfaction
Conveyed by slogans and banner-waving among marketers	Conveyed by management actions and resource commitments of key marketing executives
Seeing problems as reflections of poor marketing management	Seeing problems as opportunities for improvement in marketing systems

shirts are now available in more than 200 factory outlet stores in America as well as in discount department stores such as J. C. Penney.[7]

Figure E-1 offers a summary checklist of key concepts contained in this epilogue. Figure E-2 contrasts what process improvement emphatically is not with what it is. As Figure E-2 demonstrates, Zero-Defect Marketing represents a new way of thinking about and then managing marketing processes. It is structured, systematic, continuous, team-driven, and proactively oriented to opportunities. It is only from such fundamental mind-set and practice shifts that real progress will emerge in boosting marketing cycle time, yield, and the capacity of its systems, while simultaneously cutting waste and the unit costs of marketing activities.

Notes

1. "Frito Lay Changes Recipes for Two Top Potato Chip Brands in the U.S.A.," *Marketing News* (June 8, 1992), p. 9.
2. "The Cracks in Quality," *The Economist* (April 18, 1992), p. 67.
3. Brian Dumaine, "Closing the Innovation Gap," *Fortune* (December 2, 1991), p. 58.
4. George Stalk, Philip Evans, and Lawrence Shulman, "Competing on Capabilities: The New Rules of Corporate Strategy," *Harvard Business Review* (March-April 1992), p. 67.
5. Peter Newcomb, "All Dressed Up," *Forbes* (February 3, 1992), p. 108.
6. John Toresko, "Hewlett-Packard Keeps Reinventing Itself," *Industry Week* (August 19, 1991), p. 51.
7. "Phillips-VanHeusen's Dress Shirt Brand Has 9.9 Percent Market Share," *The Wall Street Journal* (New Jersey) (May 22, 1992), pp. B1, B5.

Index